BALLADS
OF OLD NEW YORK

ARTHUR GUITERMAN

has also written:

DEATH AND GENERAL PUTNAM, AND
101 OTHER POEMS
GAILY THE TROUBADOUR
I SING THE PIONEER
A POET'S PROVERBS
SONG AND LAUGHTER

Published by
E. P. DUTTON & CO., INC.

Ballads of Old New York

By Arthur Guiterman

Illustrated by ~ J. Scott Williams

E. P. DUTTON & COMPANY, INC.

• New York •

The author acknowledges with thanks the
courtesy of the editors of *Life, Everybody's
Magazine, Harper's Magazine,* the *New
York Times,* the *Youth's Companion, Woman's
Home Companion, House and Garden,*
the *New York World, McClure's Magazine*
and the *New York Tribune* in granting permission
to reprint many of the ballads and
lyrics in this collection.

INTRODUCTION

As a New York schoolboy, besides playing baseball and shinny in vacant lots according to the custom of my generation, I swam in our waters in summer, skated in winter wherever ice might be available, and bicycled on the old high wheel over what were then country lanes in the upper part of the island. When but a little older, I rowed up the Harlem, battled through the mill race of the Spuyten Duyvil that foamed under old King's Bridge, and drew my shell up on shore under the huge tulip tree in the cove at Inwood where I often spent long hours in a glade then all my own and as wild as it was when Henry Hudson sailed near, exploring the river that bears his name. I remember my thrill when, following what I rightly guessed to be the march of the invading Hessians, I stumbled into the unmarked trenches of Fort Tryon, discovered for myself the outworks of Fort Washington, and found the heavy lead bullet of the Revolution in earth beside the flint arrowhead of the Weckquaesgeek. So it was that I felt, as well as knew from printed records, that below the evident New York of towering buildings and crowded streets, there lie significant historic strata—the lively town of English colonial days, the Dutch village of Nieuw Amsterdam behind the palisades of Wall Street, and, under them all, the memory of that lovely Island of Manhattan, rimmed by clean waters, ridged by steep, wooded hills, jeweled with little ponds, and bright with clear brooks running through shadowy glades and sunny meadows innocent of architecture other than the rude shelters of roving Indians.

I realized that the essential character of the city is due to its almost forgotten past. From Holland, the refuge of the oppressed of Europe, the founders brought the principle of liberty of conscience that made their little settlement in turn a refuge for exiles from other colonies as well as from foreign ports. As early as 1643, when the population of the infant metropolis was less than fifteen hundred, the Director-General could say that there were "eighteen different languages" spoken in the market place. Presumably, then as now the first question that one inhabitant of Manhattan asked on meeting another, was, "Where did you come from?"

The next wave of settlement, English, Scotch and Irish, brought a new spirit of enterprise. It was the resultant combination of liberalism and adventure that stimulated the rapid growth of the city after the Revolution. A center that offers opportunity with a fair field and no favor, always draws to itself vigor and talent.

However, these ballads did not spring from any desire to moralize. I wrote them because I thought that others might share my own interest in the legendary and historic incidents on which they are based, and because I felt that our rapidly changing city has been uniquely neglectful of a past that is exceptionally varied and colorful.

The first edition of this collection was dedicated "to the valiant and happy memory of those three good New Yorkers, Peter Stuyvesant, Washington Irving and Theodore Roosevelt." Looking forward as well as backward, I re-dedicate this new edition not only to them but also to the courageous, far-seeing men and women who are establishing for the future the enduring tradition of making the city we love, ever greater, brighter and nobler.

ARTHUR GUITERMAN

January 1939

CONTENTS

DUTCH PERIOD

ILLUSTRATIONS

VOORREDE

(*Prologue*)

STEENDAM the Poet (whom all men know)
Cuddled his fiddle and poised the bow;
Quoth'a, "True lovers of tales of sprites,
Goblins and phantoms that walk o' nights,
Battles and pirates and pleasant nooks,
Quaint, homely legends from musty books,
Hear! for I carol in lilting rhymes
Rollicking lays of the Good Old Times!"

Dutch
Period

HUDSON'S VOYAGE

"A VERY good land to fall with and a pleasant
land to see." Thus wrote Mate Robert Juet
in description of the region of broken islands and
rocky hills bordering the deep harbor into which
the *Half Moon* plowed her way on the 3d of
September, 1609. Five months earlier the *Half
Moon* had sailed from Amsterdam to search for a
passage to India by the northeast; but, baffled by
headwinds and the ice and cold of Nova Zembla
and the consequent dissensions among his crew,
her experienced navigator, Master Henry Hudson,
had changed her course about, steering westward
for the shores of the New World.

After a long coasting trip, south and north
again, Hudson entered New York Bay. Hoping
that the broad channel of the river that now bears

his name might prove to be the long-sought passage to the Orient, he followed the stream beyond the present site of Albany; then, seeing that the search was fruitless, he returned to report his momentous discoveries.

HUDSON'S VOYAGE

"THROUGH the ice of Nova Zembla, through the
    fogs that held us long,
  We had sought the Northeast fairway till a head-
    wind blowing strong
  Bade us swing the kicking rudder; and we filled
    and bore away
  Ever Westward for a passage to the portals of
    Cathay.

"And we sailed o'er seas uncharted, rolling black
    and green and blue,
  Till we hailed the coastal ranges of the world
    they call the New!

[7]

And we saw a wooded headland rising boldly on
our lee—
'Twas a goodly land to fall with and a pleasant
land to see—
Where an ocean channel broadened to a hill-
encompassed bay,
And I deemed it was the highroad to the treasures of Cathay.

"There we moored our vessel safely from the
swirling autumn tides,
And the Red Men in their shallops came and
stroked her salty sides;
As they marveled at her hugeness of our friend-
ship they were fain,
And they brought us pipes of copper, mellow
grapes, and yellow grain.
When I questioned them for tidings of our
much-desired goal,
Though their savage tongue I knew not, yet they
beckoned toward the Pole.
So we heaved the *Half Moon's* anchor and we
got her under way,
And we shaped our voyage Northward for the
harbors of Cathay.

[8]

"Fifty leagues we drew a furrow on that water-
way unknown,
Past the bowered outer islands, under cliffs of
living stone,
Skirting sunlit fields that billowed to the shores
of inland seas,
Under shadowed rocky ranges with their crests of
noble trees,
Till the channel shoaled and narrowed in a
reach of highland plain,
And the brackish water sweetened—and we knew
our quest was vain.
'Twas the River of the Mountains, where the
silver salmon play;
And o'er yet untraversed waters lies the passage
to Cathay.

"So, aboard again, my trusties! for the spirit will
not rest;
We must find the golden passage, be it East or
be it West.
With a seaman's craft and courage, with a
single heart and soul,
We shall search that ocean fairway from the
Tropics to the Pole.

Yet, when softly lap the surges, in my cabin I
    may dream
Of the mighty mountain river, of that broadly
    rolling stream,
Where I heard the hum of nations in the whis-
    per of the shrouds,
While, as breath of future cities, rose the white
    September clouds.
What is all the dazzling treasure that the jew-
    eled East may give
To our new-discovered countries where the sons
    of men shall live!
But the offshore breezes freshen and the tide-
    rush will not stay;
So unmoor, and set the tiller for the sea-road
    to Cathay!"

HUDSON

Ma-hican-ittuck!
River of the Mountains,
Poured to the sea
From Adirondack crags,
Buoying the leafy
Tribute of your fountains,
Rocking the navies
Of a hundred flags!

Forests are yours,
And fair embowered islands;

[11]

Cities are yours
  Whose towers touch the skies.
Curve grandly down
  Your goblin-haunted Highlands;
Lave, golden-waved,
  The vale where Irving lies.

Deep-breasted stream,
  What tales your hills have told me!
Playmate and friend
  In days of youthful glow,
Now, as of old,
  In crystal arms enfold me;
Take me again
  Within your cooling flow!

Plunging, I watch
  Your deeper waters changing
Gold-lighted green
  To amethystine shade;
Strong-armed and free,
  Your boundless bosom ranging,
My heart in yours
  Beats warm and unafraid.

DUTCHMAN'S BREECHES

JUST after the starry flowers of the hepatica
have appeared among the dead leaves, yet before the violets have come, the wooded spaces on
and near the Island of Manhattan are beautified
with innumerable clusters of quaint little white-
and-yellow blossoms known to the schoolmen as
Dicentra cucullaria; but the children, ever quick
to recognize true resemblances, call them "Dutch-

man's breeches." That this name is not due to a mere chance resemblance is shown by this tale of the founding of a great city which will be found, in part, confirmed in the chronicles of the immortal Diedrich Knickerbocker.

Bowling Green is believed to have been the scene of that first great land purchase with which the true history of New York properly begins.

DUTCHMAN'S BREECHES

A May-Day Legend of Mannahatta

'TWAS in the month when lilacs bloom,
When apple-blossoms breathe perfume
To call the bees; when bluebirds throng,
When bobolink regains his song;
When, clear and cloudless, archly smile
The dear blue skies that love our isle.

Across a dimpling, dancing bay
That laved its bows with golden spray,
Full-sailed, a little squadron bore
To Mannahatta's virgin shore

[15]

A city's founders—Kips, Van Dorns,
Van Tienhovens, Schermerhorns,
Van Dams, Van Wycks, Van Dycks, Van Pelts,
And Onderdoncks and Roosevelts.

Right glad they leaped ashore—when lo!
With threatening spear, and supple bow
In menace bent, a stately band
Of woodland chieftains barred the strand.
"In peace return!" a sachem old
Began; "This bowered isle we hold
As sacred—ever blessed anew
By footprints of the Manitou;
Nor may we yield, for blood or spoil,
Our birthright in its hallowed soil."

Rejoined that man of subtle wit
The wily Peter Minuit,
"Hail, noble chiefs! Your island's fame
Hath reached the land from whence we came,
Wide leagues away. But little space
We crave—a meager resting-place.
Behold these keen-edged knives; this store
Of well-barbed hooks and beads galore;

These blankets and this fragrant cask!
For all, a poor exchange we ask:
The scanty plot of countryside
A Dutchman's breeches serve to hide!"

The chief assented with a smile—
(Alas! unskilled in Paleface guile!)
Then, loyal to his leader's look,
Advanced the sturdy Gert Ten Broeck—
Through Holland noted far and near
For amplitude of nether gear—
And spread, amid a hush profound,
His mighty garment on the ground!

Perhaps the wonder came to pass
By grace of good Saint Nicholas;
Perhaps a marvelous array
The Dutchman wore—I cannot say;
But, while the Red Men stared, dismayed,
Ten Broeck, in silence, stripped and laid
His mystic garments, row on row,
Until to Spuyten Duyvil's flow
A cloud of knickerbockers quite
Obscured the soil from mortal sight!

And thus our cherished dwelling-place
Was ransomed from the savage race.

For proof you ask? Ah, skeptic few!
Will Nature's word suffice for you?
Attend! When flower-laden May
Is ushered in by Moving Day,
And all our folk, with van and stage,
Renew the ancient pilgrimage—
Where still, unchained by steel and stone,
The Gentle Goddess holds her own,
Appear on clustered stems a clan
Of dancing blossoms, known to man
As "Dutchman's Breeches"—in the style
Of Sixteen-Twenty. Thus our isle
Again displays in every nook
The garments of the great Ten Broeck.

AN APRIL ROMANCE

The crystal spears of slantwise-driven Rain
    Right gallantly assail the churlish Mold
That in his frozen fastness doth enchain
    The Princess Daffodil, of trembling gold.
3

THE LEGEND OF THE BRONX

AMONG the earliest settlers north of the Haar-lem was Jonas Bronck, a well-to-do Danish Lutheran who arrived about 1640. He chose for his plantation a goodly tract bordering the quiet stream then and thereafter known as "Bronck's Kill," but by the Indians called "Ah-qua-hung," which some interpret "Place of peace"—a name that seems to have been echoed in the early title of Westchester village, "Vredeland," or "Land of Peace." The old native name acquired a new significance in 1642 when the disastrous war with the Wecquaesgeek Indians was ended by the sign-ing of a treaty of peace in the house that Jonas Bronck had built.

The learned Steendam has preserved a legend of the miraculous way in which the father of the new settlement was drawn to the site of his future home, a legend no less authentic than the cherished tales of the founding of Thebes, Carthage, and Rome.

THE LEGEND OF THE BRONX

With sword and Bible, brood and dame,
Across the seas from Denmark came
Stout Jonas Bronck. He roved among
The wooded vales of Ah-qua-hung.
"Good sooth! on every hand," quoth he,
"Are pleasant lands and fair to see;
But which were best to plow and till
And meetest both for manse and mill?"

"Bronck! Bronck! Bronck!"
  Called the frogs from the reeds of the river;
"Bronck! Bronck! Bronck!"
  From the marshes and pools of the stream.
"Here let your journeyings cease;
  Blest of the Bounteous Giver,
Yours is the Valley of Peace,
  Here is the home of your dream."

"Oho!" laughed Jonas Bronck; "I ween
These pop-eyed elves in bottle-green

Do call my name to show the spot
Predestined!—Here I cast my lot!"
So there he reared his dwelling-place
And built a mill, with wheel and race.
And even now, beneath the hill
When summer nights are fair and still:

"Bronck! Bronck! Bronck!"
　Rise the cadenced batrachian numbers;
"Bronck! Bronck! Bronck!"
　Chant a myriad chorister gnomes;
"High on the shadowy crest
　Under the hemlock he slumbers.
Here is the region of rest;
　Come to our Valley of Homes!"

THE CRITICS

The moon was up and I was young:
No matter what I dared to write,
But how it woke each sportive tongue
Of little elves that haunt the night!

Though Crickets chanted, "True, true, true!"
  The Tree Toads piped, "'Tis not! 'Tis not!"
The Hermit Howlet jeered, "Hoo! hoo!"
  And Gaffer Bullfrog blurted, "Rot!"

So, red with wrath, I flung the scrawl
  Across the walk—and lo! by day.
The Dew, the truest friend of all,
  Had washed those erring lines away.

———

RAMBOUT VAN DAM

NOW this, the legend of the Flying Dutchman of the Tappan Zee—the broad reach of the Hudson at Tarrytown—is entitled to particular respect as a double-barreled tract against profanity and Sabbath-breaking. Any one who chooses to follow by rowboat Rambout's course from the mouth of the Spuyten Duyvil up the river about as far as Nyack will have (in addition to blistered hands) a great respect for the hero's prowess as an oarsman.

"Zee" should really be pronounced as if spelled "Zay"; but the popular pronunciation, which is in accordance with the actual spelling, has been adopted in this and subsequent ballads as being that which is likely to prevail.

RAMBOUT VAN DAM

THE FLYING DUTCHMAN OF THE TAPPAN ZEE

ON Tappan Zee a shroud of gray
   Is heavy, dank, and low;
All dimly gleams the beacon-ray
   Of White Pocantico.

No skipper braves old Hudson now
   Where Nyack's headlands frown,
And safely moored is every prow
   Of drowsy Tarrytown;

Yet, clear as word of human lip,
   The river sends its shores
The rhythmic rullock-clank and drip
   Of even-rolling oars.

What rower plies a reckless oar
  With mist on flood and strand?
That oarsman toils for evermore,
  And ne'er shall reach the land!

———

Roistering, rollicking Ram van Dam,
Fond of a frolic and fond of a dram,
Fonder—yea, fonder, proclaims Renown,
Of Tryntje Bogardus of Tarrytown,
Leave Spuyten Duyvil to roar his song!
Pull! for the current is sly and strong;
Nestles the robin and flies the bat.
Ho! for the frolic at Kakiat!
Merry the sport at the quilting-bee
Held at the farm by the Tappan Zee!
Jovial labor with quips and flings
Dances with wonderful pigeonwings,
Twitter of maidens and clack of dames,
Honest flirtations and rousing games;
Platters of savory beef and brawn,
Buckets of treacle and good suppawn,
Oceans of cider and beer in lakes,
Mountains of crullers and honey-cakes—

Such entertainment should never pall!
Rambout van Dam took his fill of all;
Laughed with the wittiest, worked with a zest,
Danced with the prettiest, drank with the best.

Oh, that enjoyment should breed annoy!
Tryntje grew fickle, or cold or coy;
Rambout, possessed of a jealous sprite,
Scowled like the sky on a stormy night,
Snarled a "good-by" from his sullen throat,
Blustered away to his tugging boat.
After him hastened Jacobus Horn:
"Stay with us, Rambout, till Monday morn.
Soon in the east will the dawn be gray;
Rest from thy oars on the Sabbath Day."
Angrily, Rambout van Dam ripped back:
"Dunder en blixem! du Schobbejak!
Preach to thy children! and let them know
Spite of the Duyvil and thee, I'll row
Thousands of Sundays, if need there be,
Home o'er this ewig-vervlekte zee!"
Muttering curses, he headed south.
Jacob, astounded, with open mouth
Watched him receding, when—crash on crash
Volleyed the thunder! A hissing flash

Smote on the river!—He looked again:—
Rambout was gone from the sight of men!

Old Dunderberg with grumbling roar
    Hath warned the fog to flee,
But still that never-wearied oar
    Is heard on Tappan Zee.

A moon is closed in Hudson's breast
    And lanterns gem the town;
The phantom craft that may not rest
    Plies ever, up and down,

'Neath skies of blue and skies of gray,
    In spite of wind or tide,
Until the trump of Judgment Day;—
    A sound—and naught beside.

EIGHT OARS AND A COXSWAIN

Eight oars compel
Our darting shell,
Eight oar-blades flash the sun;
The hard arms thrill,
The deep lungs fill,
Eight backs are bent as one.
All silver lined
We leave behind
Each wave of somber hue.
"Stroke! Stroke!
Stroke! Stroke!
Steady, Number Two!"

The sea-gulls go,
A drift of snow,
On Hudson's lights and shades;
The eagle swings
On splendid wings
Above the Palisades.
Let Caution steer
The shore anear,
But Valor takes the tide.
"Stroke! Stroke!
Stroke! Stroke!
Ease your forward slide!"

A fair league still
To old Cock Hill,
Where Spuyten Duyvil roars.
No time for play;
Give 'way; give 'way!
And bend the driven oars!
When breezes blow
Then feather low
With level blades and true.
"Stroke! Stroke!
Stroke! Stroke!
Steady! Pull it thr-o-o-ough!"

[31]

HOW PEARL STREET WAS PAVED

ALTHOUGH the statement has been made as a jest and is generally regarded as such, it is nevertheless literally true that several of the old streets of New York were originally laid out by the public-spirited cows of the settlers. An instance of this primitive method of road-engineering exists in crooked old Pearl Street, the lower part of which formed the original water-front of New Amsterdam on the east. This street, thus almost miraculously created, received its first pavement in a manner likewise so happy (and economical) as to justify both the burghers of old and their modern successors in trusting to Providence for the furtherance of public improvements.

HOW PEARL STREET WAS PAVED

In Wouter Van Twiller's manorial pale
There flourished a cow (and she flourished a tail)
Safe-housed, where the Battery guarded the shore
In kindly communion with many cows more.
Awaking from visions of clover, each morn
She drowsily lowed to the drover whose horn
Was blown at each byre; then, leading the line
Of sleepy New Amsterdam's somnolent kine,
She sauntered with Sukey and Brindle and all
Away to the Common beyond the Town Wall.

The route that she plodded by hillock and stream
Was crookedly quaint as a summer night's dream;
For, though at the start, like an orderly beast,
She skirted the river that flows on the east,

Soon, tempted by boskage and cress of the best,
She rambled and browsed to the north or the west;
Till, trodden each morning and evening, there
    showed
A devious pathway that wore to a road
Where brick-fronted houses began to appear
To crown the caprice of that "Boss" engineer.
(And this is the cause of the intricate way
The streets of New Amsterdam wander to-day.)

Next, keen for progression, the burghers decreed
The street should be paved with the uttermost
    speed,
And chose a committee of good men and true
To think out the problem and put the thing
    through.
Van Bommel, Van Keuren, Hans Jacobson Kol,
Claes Tysen, Joost Smeeman, and Huybertsen Mol,
All stout at the trencher and wise in debate,
Held council portentous both early and late.

They grouped on the road at the first flush of dawn
With pipes of tobacco and bowls of suppawn
And dreamed of all pavings that ever were known—
Block, corduroy, cement, gold, mortar, and stone.

[34]

And ever they puffed as they pondered, and quaffed,
To clear their perceptions, full many a draught,
And dined on the oysters .

And ever they puffed as they pondered, and quaffed,
To clear their perceptions, full many a draught,
And dined on the oysters abounding of yore
In numberless shoals on our fortunate shore.
(The bivalves our fathers deemed worthy of praise
Were giants that mock these degenerate days;
For find me an oyster, in bay, creek, or foss
To-day, that will measure twelve inches across!)

A fortnight they tarried to feast and perpend,
Surveying the road from beginning to end;
When lo! what a mountain of labor was saved;
For, e'en as they feasted, the road had been paved,
And paved for the tread of a prince or an earl
With oyster-shells, brilliant in mother-of-pearl!
So "Pearl" was the name, undeniably meet,
The burghers bestowed on that marvelous street.

'Twas thus that our city's progenitors showed
The very best method of paving a road:
Appoint a committee to dally and doubt
And somehow the matter will work itself out.
So, taught by experience, that is the way
We manage the streets of the city to-day.

[37]

AN OLD ROAD

In days that were—no matter when—
'Twas not a weed-grown palindrome,
At either end a dreamy glen,
But led, like other roads, to Rome.

Its dust was ridged by many wheels
That rolled to market, church, and fair;
But now a wave of grass conceals
The road that leads not anywhere.

The chipmunk haunts its tumbled walls
Where roses wait the wild-bee's kiss,
And honeysuckle droops and falls
Entwined with ropes of clematis.

And here the nesting meadow-lark
Hath built; and wisps of maidenhair
O'er-veil the grooves that faintly mark
The road that leads not anywhere.

[38]

Because it bore the grinding jar
   Of sullen wheels from year to year,
Its twilight owns a softer star—
   A sweeter silence lingers here.

And we, outworn by toil and stress,
   As truant urchins let us fare,
Like our dear pathway, purposeless—
   The road that leads not anywhere.

THE LORD OF THE DUNDERBERG

WHEN the *Goede Vrouw* discharged upon our shores her load of hearty Dutch settlers, she also let loose a horde of old-world sprites and goblins, elvish stowaways, who, unknown to captain or crew, had followed the fortunes of their mortal fellow-countrymen to the New World. These were no flimsy-winged sylphs and fairies, idling away their time slumbering in roses or dancing on the green. Honest, homely Robin Goodfellows were they all, delighting in useful labor and rough sport; benevolent, yet prone to mischief; friends to man, but jealously exacting from him all traditional dues of tribute and honor. Well fitted to cope with the ruggedness of an untamed land, they spread rapidly through the valley of the Hudson, peopling its glens with their hardy brood.

The chieftain of the most powerful of these goblin clans was the Heer or Lord of the Dunderberg. His dominions extended through the Highlands of the Hudson from the Dunderberg or Thunder Mountain, commanding the perilous

[40]

strait of the Devil's Race, at the south, to Pollopel (which means "Soupladle") Island that lies in the Wind Gate, as the northern entrance to the enchanted region is known. This potentate, while by no means of a malignant disposition, was exceedingly tenacious of his prerogatives; and woe betide the skipper who neglected to pay homage by lowering his flag on entering the domain of him who had at his command all the gales and tempests that lay snugly tucked away in the recesses of the hills!

THE LORD OF THE DUNDERBERG

GOBLIN and kobold and elf and gnome
Riot and rollick and make their home
Deep in the Highlands, where Hudson glides,
Curving the sweep of his volumed tides
Round wooded islet and granite base
Down through the rush of the Devil's Race.
Great is the prowess of Goblin might;
Dread is the malice of troll and sprite;
Chief of them all is the potent Dwerg,
Heer of the Keep of the Dunderberg!

Mountain and River obey his spell
E'en to the Island of Pollopel;
Brooding, he sits in the rugged glen,
Jealous of honor of sprites and men.
Ye who would sail his dominions through
Scatheless, withhold not the homage due!
Lower your peak and its flaunting flag!
Strike!—to the Lord of the Thunder Crag!

Gracefully rounded and broad of beam,
Breasting the calms of the golden stream,
Slanting along o'er the Tappan Rack,
Sidled the *Geertruyd van Haagensack.*
Sometimes she wobbled, for, be it told,
Casked in the darks of her roomy hold
Gurgled the liquor of pleasant sin—
Rum of Jamaica and Holland's gin!

Puffing his pipe on the after-deck
Glowered the captain, Gerardus Keck—
Sour and headstrong, but stout of soul,
Scorner of legends of spuke and troll.
Up came the boatswain with pallid face:
"Captain! we swing in the Devil's Race!

Will ye not lower the orange flag
Here, in the shade of the Thunder Crag?
"Dikkop! Bemoeial!" the captain roared;
"Durfniet! the wrath of thy Goblin Lord
Lightly I hold as a stoup of rum!
Broom to the masthead!—and let 'em come!"

Shrouding the vessel, before they wist,
Streamed from the Mountain a curdling mist.
Piercing the woof of that leaden veil
Pelted and rattled the heavy hail.
Hudson arose like a tortured snake,
Foaming and heaving; the thunder spake,
Rolled from the cliffs, and the lightning played
Viciously red through the pallid shade!

Oh! how the elements howled and wailed!
Oh! how the crew of the *Geertruyd* quailed,
Huddling together with starting eyes!
For, in the rack, like a swarm of flies,
Legions of goblins in doublet and hose
Gamboled and frolicked off Anthony's Nose;
While on the shuddering masthead sat
Cross-leggèd, crowned with his steeple-hat,
Grinning with mischief, that potent Dwerg,
Lord of the Keep of the Dunderberg!

Wild was the laughter that quaking men
Heard through the night from the Goblin Glen.

Brawled o'er the gunwale the frothing tide.
"Up with the cargo!" the captain cried;
"Lighten the vessel or else we sink!"
Over the side went the precious drink!
Darting like swallows, those goblin knaves
Caught up the casks ere they touched the waves.
Back to their mountains the thievish crew
Whirled with their booty; before them flew,
Waving in triumph a captured flag,
He of the Heights of the Thunder Crag!

Gone was the tempest! With sails adroop,
Battered and draggled, the plundered sloop,
Stemming a current without a swell,
Crept past the Island of Pollopel.
Wild was the laughter that quaking men
Heard through the night from the Goblin Glen
Where, in a revel, the gleeful horde
Drank to the fame of their puissant Lord!

Skippers that scoff when the sky is bright,
Heed ye this story of goblin might!
Strange the adventures of barks that come
Laden with cargoes of gin and rum!
  When the Storm Ship drives with her head to gale
  And the corpse-light gleams in her hollow sail—

When Cro' Nest laughs in the tempest's hem
While the lightnings weave him a diadem—
When Storm King shouts through the spumy
    wrack
And Bull Hill bellows the thunder back—
Beware of the wrath of the mighty Dwerg!
Strike flag to the Lord of the Dunderberg!

THUNDER-STORM

The smiths of the heavens are mending the weather;
Their hammers are beating the fragments together.
The cumulus mountains with nebulous gorges
Are dazzled with flame of the wind-bellowsed forges;
The cloud-pillared anvils with silvery edges
Resound to the thunderous fall of the sledges;
Till broadening patches of azure are showing
Storm-welded, rain-tempered, and, splendidly glow-
*   ing,*
The rainbow, from valley to valley extended,
Proclaims to the world that the weather is mended.

[49]

A LEGEND OF MAIDEN LANE

TO this day the narrow, devious line of Maiden Lane follows the course of the lost rivulet in whose clear pool the maidens of New Amsterdam were wont to wash the family linen, and along whose wooded banks they often strolled on summer evenings with the right sort of company. The abrupt ascent of the land along Nassau Street to the southward preserves the memory of the steep hill on the crest of which stood Jan Vinge's windmill, while the more gradual slope to the north commemorates the Klaaver Waytie, or clover meadow of the Jan Jansen Damen farm.

Of all the romances that cluster around "T' Maegde-Padtje," or "The Maiden's Path," none is of greater interest than that preserved in the records of an old New York family, which tell how the founder of the house was once in that green lane sorely tempted of the devil, of how he was strengthened to resist temptation, and of the good fortune that was granted him.

5

A LEGEND OF MAIDEN LANE

'TWAS dusk in the dale, but the clover-clad hill
Was rosy in twilight; the sails of the mill
Were moving slow shadows o'er hillocks of corn
And barley; the cadence of Gabriel's horn—
Old Gabriel Cropsey's—proclaimed to his cows
The close of their hour to idle and browse;
When, down the deep vale that the rivulet made
A gladness of shallow and rill and cascade,
There tramped a tall youth in a study profound,
His hands in his pockets, his eyes on the ground,

Unheeding the buttercups raised for the dew,
Unheeding the herdsman's full-throated halloo,
Unheeding the large-eyed reproach of the cows.
The droop of the hat o'er the puckering brows,
The stoop of the shoulders and head, made it clear
That something was ailing with Corny van Leer.

Yes, something was wrong; he was weary and sore
With drudging long hours, unthanked, in the store
Of Steenwyck the merchant, who smoked in his
    chair,
Whose coffers were brimming as Corny's were bare,
Who dined like—a burgher, whose garments were
    brave.
"The man who is poor might as well be a slave!"
Groaned Corny. "Why toil till you're wrinkled
    and gray,
With wealth all around one? There must be a way!
Suppose—" "Ah, suppose!" purred a voice in his
    ear
So gently that Corny scarce wondered to hear
That echo. He turned; and he saw, or he dreamed,
A tall, swarthy Person, whose jetty eyes gleamed
Quite kindly. A beaver he wore on his head;
His cloak and his doublet were sable and red;

His breeches (of brimstone) seemed meagerly lined,
And yet they projected most queerly behind!

"Suppose, my good lad" (ah! those accents were
        bland!)—
"Suppose, my dear Corny, you had at command
A few paltry guilders? What wealth could be
        made
By dabbling a bit in the Indian trade!
Now look ye! Old Steenwyck has silver to spare,
And most of it won by your labor, I'll swear;
Suppose that you borrow a handful or so
A fortnight? I warrant you, he'll never know;
And—trust me, I've proved it too often to doubt—
The one thing that's wrongful is being found out.
Besides, when you've made eighty guilders of ten
(I'll show you the way), you'll repay them again.

"So"— Hark! what a melody toned in his ear!
What rich, golden laughter, so merry and clear
That bluebird and oriole wakened, and sang
A duo to answer the copse whence it rang!
It rose like a fountain that bursts through the snow;
It fell like the waterfall bubbling below;

'Twas thrushes and bobolinks greeting the sun
That shines through the raindrops when showers
    are done;
A breath of the hills to the mist-clouded plain,
It swept the black fog from his heart and his brain.
Clear-eyed and erect, to the Shape at his right
He turned—but the Tempter had vanished from
    sight!

Still rippling with merriment, out from the dell
Of hazels came Maritje Bleecker to tell
How, seeing a youth who was everywhere known
For gladness and jollity, brooding alone
In gloomy despair of the somberest hue,
She laughed, as who wouldn't? He'd better laugh,
    too!

An ocean of silver the heavens poured down
On the queer, gabled roofs of our dear, fabled town
As, home through the meadows, in moonlight
    and shade,
They wandered together, a man and a maid.
But all that was spoken the world may not know;
The pathways were narrow, their voices were low,

[55]

And no one o'erheard but the Crickets and Elves;
That's all. You may finish the story yourselves.

Yet, this is to add; 'tis a maxim of cheer
Preserved in the tomes of the House of Van Leer:
"Of Naught is ye Duyvil soe deeply affray'd
As a sweete, wholesome Laugh from ye Hearte of
    a Mayde!"

A SONG IN JUNE

On a rosebush that grows in the garden you love
   There are three opening buds on a single green
      stem;
And they dream as they nod to your window above
   That it would not be June if it were not for them.

There's an oriole brave as a prince on his throne
   In his orange-and-black in the mulberry-tree.
As he flutes to a world that he knows for his own,
   "Oh, it would not be June if it were not for me!"

Let the oriole sing to the earth and the sky,
  And the roses unfold to the kiss of the dew!
But the light of my soul is the glance of your eye,
  And it would not be June if it were not
    for you.

THE RATTLE-WATCH OF NEW
AMSTERDAM

EVEN in quiet New Amsterdam laws were made
to be broken, and as a corollary it was needful
to establish a police force. The code that required
enforcement included ordinances against fast driving, against shooting game within the city limits,
against fighting with knives, against allowing pigs
and goats to roam unrestrained through the metro-
politan streets, as well as regulations governing
the liquor traffic.

The police force consisted of a Ratelwacht of
six men who were required to go about the city
at night calling out the hour, evidently so that
sleeping citizens might know it was not yet time
to wake, and sounding their rattles, presumably
to give the evil-intentioned due warning of their
approach.

Among the many regulations prescribing what
these guardians of the peace should and should not
do was one providing that: "Whatever any of the

[59]

Watch shall get from any of the prisoners, whether lock-up money, present or other fee, which those of the Watch shall receive by consent of the Burgomasters, it shall be brought into the hands of the Captain for the benefit of the fellow-watchmen and shall be there preserved until divided around." A worthy rule, doubtless as rigorously followed in those early times as to-day.

The Rattle-Watch of New Amsterdam.

THE RATTLE-WATCH OF NEW AMSTERDAM

"Rrr! — Rrr! — Rrr! — Rrr!"

Hark to the rattle's discordant swell!
"Ten is the hour and all is well!"
Musket on shoulder and dirk on thigh,
Forth from the fort, with a soulful sigh,
Wiping their lips of a parting dram,
Sally the Watch of New Amsterdam.
Smite with your rattles the startled ear!
Let every miscreant know you're near.
Bellow the hour to the sentry moon!
Some honest burgher might wake too soon.
Come, merry lover of sights and sounds,
Follow the Watch on their nightly rounds!

Marching as though to the roll of drums,
Here little Stoffel the tailor comes,
Drunk as a hero on musty ale,
Waving an arm like a windmill sail,

[63]

Threat'ning our lives with his weighty goose!
Bundle him off to the calaboose!

"Hola! Friend Watchman!" "Well, what's the
    need?"
"Sailors afighting! Oh, come with speed!—
Fighting with knives on the Water Street!"
"Down on the river? That's off my beat;
You go, young Joris; yet, hark ye, boy,
Meddling with tars is a mad employ.
Wait till they've done, like a youth of brains,
Then, to the lock-up with what remains!"

"Ho, Doktor Kierstede! I take my vow
Here on the highway I find thy sow,
Never a ring in her nose, I say,
Rooting the road in a shameful way,
Plainly defying the statute—" (Clink!)
"Hsh! here's the captain!—No, I don't drink,
Not while on duty; it isn't right.
(Thank ye, Heer Doktor.) Good night! Good
    night!"

"Softly! We'll capture the wicked wight!
You to the left, Dirck, and Jan to right,
[64]

Pieter in front of him, I behind!
Ha! have we caught thee, thou varlet blind?
Little thou thoughtest our eyes would mark
Stealers of cabbages in the dark!
Now in the pillory shalt thou stand
Holding a cabbage in either hand,
Yea, and a third on thy cabbage head—
Thief of the Dominie's cabbage-bed!"

Thus in the days that are called "of yore,"
Terror of caitiffs, a gallant corps
Guarded our city for noble pay:
Twenty-four stuyvers per night or day
(Forty-eight cents to our modern thrift),
One or two beavers by way of gift,
And, in the winter, 'twas understood,
Three hundred fagots of firewood.
Wouldn't it stagger the budget-roll
If our patrolmen were paid in coal!

MINETTA WATER

(The Song of the Buried Stream)

Deer-hoof dint and moccasin print
  Stamped the moss that rimmed my flow;
Adder's-tongue and fragrant mint
  Grew—where nothing now may grow;

Dragon-flies in shimmering schools
  Reveled here, an airy rout;
Minnows rilled my glimmering pools,
  Through my rapids flashed the trout.

Gone the hunter, fled the deer;
  All the birds I loved are flown;
Men have hid my waters clear
  Under piles of rigid stone.

Men have tombed my silver springs;
  Yet, within the sunless caves
All unheard my torrent sings,
  All unseen I pour my waves.

[66]

Mocking, delving, deep I lurk.
  What! they dream my fount is dry?
Lo! I ruin all their work.
  Mortal, they; but deathless, I.

Let them hold their gloomy day!
  I that laugh shall rule at last.
When the massive walls decay,
  When the towers to earth are cast,

I shall flash a clearer sun,
  I shall lure my birds again;
Deep in bloom my streams shall run
  Through the crumbled homes of men.

6

SLEEPY HOLLOW

SOME day—let it be in the apple-blossom season or else in early October when the Palisades across the river are ablaze with changing leaves—make your little pilgrimage through the loveliest country in the world to the old churchyard of Tarrytown where the sunny-hearted enchanter whose spell forever hallows the valley of the Hudson lies asleep. Although time has wrought cruel changes in the neighboring town, you will find that the little secluded nook by the Pocantico is yet subject to the drowsy influence that pervaded it in the days of Geoffrey Crayon and Diedrich Knickerbocker.

In reference to the cause of the slumberous atmosphere of the Hollow the great chronicler of New Amsterdam rather dubiously observes, "Some say that the place was bewitched by a High German doctor, during the early days of the settlement; others, that an old Indian chief, the prophet or wizard of his tribe, held his powwows there."

Should any ardent controversialists quarrel in behalf of one or the other of these alternative explanations, they are like to find themselves in the plight of the two opinionated knights who met in mortal combat upon the question of whether the shield was silver or gold, only to learn as they lay dying of their wounds that one side was of the yellow metal, the other of the white. So, lest any such foul debate arise to break the sacred peace of the Hollow, do I tell this true tale of its bewitching, learned on one of many tarryings in the enchanted region.

SLEEPY HOLLOW

'TWAS in the drowsy Moon of Falling Leaves,
   And waning summer gave a softer glow,
And apples dropped, and hosts of yellow sheaves
   Were bravely tented where Pocantico

Devolves his lazy waters through the nave
   Of sunny hills, and past the silent peak
That casts a somber shadow o'er the cave
   Of Maqua, Wizard of the Wecquaesgeek—

When, up the winding way from Hudson's shore,
   Came Doktor Nebelhut, the German Sage,
To sound the fountains of forbidden lore
   In mystic council with the Forest Mage.

Above the Wizard's portal, huge and hard,
   A balanced crag had worn itself a place
When rocked by winter tempests—deeply scarred
   With dumb inscriptions of a vanished race;

[70]

And long that rugged sentinel had viewed
  The sylvan peace of Hudson's rolling glades,
The River's breadth of silver solitude,
  The furrowed grandeur of his Palisades.

Within the crypt discoursed the Sages twain,
  In fellowship of craft and eager zest
As if from one deep chalice they would drain
  The mingled wizardry of East and West—

Of charms to bring the butter to the churn,
  Of spells to call the red deer from the wold,
Love philters, incantations to discern
  The haunted hiding-place of pirate gold;

Dark, awful runes that might not be expressed,
  Dread weirds, the thought of which is deadly sin!
And now the Doktor drew from out his vest
  A quaintly fashioned pouch of cobra-skin.

"This holds," said he, "a leaf that giveth calm—
  Yea, even as thy fragrant-fuming weed—
But, blent with mandragora's potent balm
  And soothing essence of the poppy-seed,

"When I do blow its azure vapor forth
    In melting wreaths, o'er valley, plain, and hill,
Who breathes it—east or west or south or north—
    Shall droop in childlike slumber at my will!"

The Red Man's cheek was wrinkled in a smile:
    "A mighty medicine, O Friend, is thine!
And dare I tell to thee the simple wile
    We learn amid the whispers of the pine?

"Then hear!—The willow's ruddy bark I burn
    Within my pipe. Upon the coal I fling
These russet seedlets, brushed from plumes of fern
    In moonlight by the howlet's velvet wing.

"Within the bowl the crimson sparkle gleams!
    Upon the air the hazy fillets rise!
Who scents that cloud shall drowse in wondrous
    dreams,
    While I shall walk unseen of mortal eyes!"

Then half in pique, "Well spoke!" the Doktor said,
    "My swarthy Brother!—Prithee, let us show
Our magic's force!" The Wizard bowed his head.
    The pipes were lit; and upward-rolling slow

From creamy meerschaum, waif of Græcia's wave,
　　And dark red sandstone dug of prairie fells,
The heavy incense filled the narrow cave,
　　And outward surging, veiled the golden dells.

Throughout the vale, where'er that vapor crept,
　　The busy farmer dozed beside his wain;
The housewife in the dairy sighed, and slept;
　　The fisher let his line unheeded strain;

The bronze-limbed hunter slacked his arching bow;
　　The deer forgot to leap, the hawk to fly;
The lilies drooped; the hemlock nodded low,
　　And every aster closed its purple eye.

Of them that wrought the marvel?—Strange their
　　plight!
　　In vain they strove against the magic hest!
Till, smiling each to each a long "Good-night,"
　　They closed their eyes in twice-enchanted rest.

And e'en the sentry boulder knew the charm;
　　Awhile it quivered like a blade of grass,
Then, sliding softly as a sleeper's arm,
　　It sealed the cavern with its granite mass.

Around that cave the leafy creepers cling,
  Above its roof in summer, roses blow;
And o'er the mossy portal, in the spring
  The dogwood pours its avalanche of snow.

And still they doze—the necromantic twain,
  While from their pipes the witching fumes arise;
And still, when Indian Summer bows the grain,
  That eery vapor dims the tender skies.

And still the valley lies beneath a spell;
  And wondrous clouds and visions they do know
Who loiter in the dream-enchanted dell
  That hears the murmur of Pocantico.

A SPRINGTIME PILGRIMAGE

Feet on the hills and heads in the sky,
  Bathing our brows in the breath of spring,
Buoyant and youthful and clear of eye
  Over a glorified road we swing.

Meadows are greening their winter tan,
  Orchards are heavy with scented snow.
On! through the Vale of the Nepperhan,
  Over the Heights of Pocantico!

Dogwood and laurel and trailing pine
  Mantle the furrowed and craggy scaurs;
Creamy dicentra and columbine
  Nod o'er the ashes of buried wars;

Rebel and Tory have made their bed—
  Harmless, their sabers a truce have found
Under the verdure that lifts our tread,
  Deep in the heart of the Neutral Ground.

(Here is the church on the haunted ridge,
  Lichens of centuries fleck the sides;
Shrouded and headless, o'er yonder bridge
  Nightly the Galloping Hessian rides.

(What though a burden of moldered stones
  Cover their forms from the eyes of men!
Ichabod, Baltus, and Big Brom Bones
  Rise through the magic of Irving's pen.)

Hudson in majesty meets the sea—
  Monarch of mountains and goblin glades;
Laughing, the ripple of Tappan Zee
  Mocks at the frown of the Palisades.

Slumbers the land in a golden spell.
  Hush! The Enchanter hath laid him down,
Close by the river he loved so well,
  Here in the Hollow of Tarrytown.

A SCANDAL IN NEW AMSTERDAM

EVERY Saturday morning New Amsterdam was enlivened by the weekly market held at the Strand, or East River water-front, near the house of Dr. Hans Kierstede, which stood on the north side of Pearl Street and the corner of Moore Street, where were the weighing-house and the only little dock in the town.

Thither came the country-folk from Haarlem, Breuckelen, Vlissingen (Flushing), Hoboken-Hacking, Ompoge (Amboy), Ahasimus, and New Utrecht in carts, on horseback, in shallops, canoes, or market-boats which they moored in the Heere Graft or Broad Street canal, bringing their supplies of veal, pork, butter, cheese, milk, tobacco, peaches, cider, herbs, melons, oysters, shad, chickens, geese, turkeys, pelicans, eel-shovelers, and quail to exchange for linsey-woolsey cloth, medicines, arrack, sugar, ribbons, caps, and finery for Sunday wear, clay pipes and like commodities of town life, for Dutch guilders and stuyvers or for

Indian sewant or wampum which was the principal circulating medium in the days of Wilhelmus Kieft. Thither came the Indians of Long Island and the Hudson River country with venison and other game and packs of furs and skins—beaver, mink, bear, wolf, wildcat, and panther. There gathered the farmers' wives and daughters, keen for bargaining, but just as eager to exchange gossip with the ladies of the city.

In default of newspapers, all the news of the day passed from mouth to mouth; and if a few choice scandals were thus put in circulation, they were assuredly no worse than many that have been whispered at the tea-drinkings of later days. The scandal referred to in the title is embalmed in New Amsterdam's early records of litigation.

A SCANDAL IN NEW AMSTERDAM

ACROSS the inlet's ebb and rise
The spotless houses glare surprise
From all their gable-hooded eyes
  On motley, mingling craft—
The light canoe from wilds remote,
The blunt bateau and market-boat,
And shallop, dugout, skiff, and float
  Within "Die Heere Graft."

The bronze Mohegan brings the spoil
Of wood and river; what the soil
Hath yielded to his sturdy toil,
  With plaintive calf and lamb
The farmer hales in groaning dray
Along the forest-bordered way,
For this is held a market day
  In fair New Amsterdam.

Like finches, round the market-boats
The rosy vrouws, with kerchiefed throats
And short but ample petticoats

And hoods and kirtles gay,
Are gathering and scattering
And chaffering and chattering,
The Ninth Commandment shattering;
    Then hark to what they say!

"Thou coppery knave with the cloven ear!
Pray, what is thy charge for this puny deer?
Twelve stuyvers in wampum! As I'm alive
Such venison wouldn't be cheap at five!
You savages, verily, grow too bold;
Dost fancy our burghers are made of gold?
Go! Take it away to thy woods again!
Eleven thou sayest? I'll give thee ten."

"Ah, Mevrouw von Blarcom! we meet again!
What news from the village of Vlissingen?
Soh! Adrian Joostan is gone at last!
Poor man; 'tis a mercy his woes are past.
Yea? Journeyed to Hartford hath Pieter Volck!
How reckless to trust to the Yankee folk!
Nay, little of moment hath passed in town.
The governor's dame hath a silken gown.
Hast heard of the strife 'twixt our Dominie
Bogardus and Antony Jan Salee?

"Then such a commotion you never saw!
Vrouw Anneke vowed she would have the law."

"The trouble was started, so all avow,
By Anneke Jansen, the Dominie's vrouw,
Who, chatting one Saturday over her tea,
Spake somewhat unkindly of Vrouw Salee;
Mayhap that her linens were none too clean,
Her servants ill-bred, or her larder lean.
Whatever she said of her, I'll be bound
It lost not a jot as it traveled round;
And, truthful or slanderous, let that be,
It kindled the wrath of the Vrouw Salee,
Who rushed to her friends with a look intense
To tell them, in veriest confidence,
How, crossing a street of this muddy town,
Good Madam Bogardus had raised her gown—
M-m, higher than prudent. Yea, showed, indeed,
Well—more of her ankles than there was need!

"Then such a commotion you never saw!
Vrouw Anneke vowed she would have the law.
The Dominie sued for his dame (of course
Thou knowest the mare is the better horse).
The Schepens with sober and solemn face
Examined and pondered the weighty case,
And sentenced poor Madam Salee to tell
In public, at sound of the crier's bell,

7   [83]

That falsely she'd spoken—alack, the shame!—
And the Dominie's wife was a worthy dame.
Moreover, her husband hath sadly paid
Three guilders and more for his wife's tirade.

"Good faith! but our magistrates win applause,
So wisely and well they enforce the laws!
For truly the tongue is a two-edged sword,
And Slander's a monster that stalks abroad,
Devouring all with a mouth of flame;
And no one is safe from the smudge of blame.
(But—this is in confidence 'twixt us two—
I firmly believe that the tale was true!)"

KISSING BRIDGE

(Once at the junction of Roosevelt Street and Park Row.)

No Roebling reared that primal way
    With web of steel and splendid line;
Its piers were rubble, crude and gray,
    Its beams were hewn of forest pine.

Across the kill that eastward flowed
    It led, unjarred by rumbling tram,
Where grasses waved and lilies glowed;
    New York was then Nieuw Amsterdam.

With rake and scythe at droop of day,
    With lilt and carol full and free,
The maids and younkers hold their way
    Along the shadowed Bouwerie.

A playful whisper stirs the trees,
    A laughing ripple rills the shoal,
For here, as village law decrees,
    The sweetest lips must pay the toll.

[85]

Good Saint that loved our isle, restore
  That hallowed bridge, to span a tide
With blowing fields on either shore;
  Let me be there with one beside!

Dispel this cloud of stone and steel,
  These clogging mists of tawdry sham!
Let lips be frank and hearts be leal
  As then in old Nieuw Amsterdam!

Kissing Bridge

A TRIAL IN NEW AMSTERDAM

M AN is a quarrelsome animal and his social and political history is largely a record of battles and suits-at-law.

Dry as some might think them, the records of the Court of Burgomasters and Schepens of New Amsterdam contain the germs of many rare tales and are delightful in their naïve gravity. From them one may glean that the good people of the town sometimes failed to pay their taxes; that they sometimes engaged in fisticuffs; that they frequently violated the liquor laws; that they even took unfair advantage of one another in business transactions; and that they were woefully addicted to slander, backbiting, and the calling of evil names—in short, that they were very human.

As for the judgments of the primitive court, they were of the Solomonic order. Never did that worthy tribunal walk around the square in order to reach the house next door. Perhaps its decisions were not monuments of legal erudition, but they were simple, direct, and satisfying to the unscientific lay mind, and in all probability generally made for justice. Witness a case in point.

A TRIAL IN NEW AMSTERDAM

Ye who have chafed at the law's delays
And the tedious trials of later days—
Ye who have laughed at the sage pretense
That ponders ridiculous evidence—
Hear of a process, devoid of sham,
In the trim little town of New Amsterdam.

Burgher Jan Haeckius standeth here
Claiming his due for a keg of beer
Sold—on the record this fact stands proven—
To crafty Jacobus Van Couwenhouven.
Cometh Jacobus, that wily man,
Boldly admitting the sale by Jan,
Natheless maintaining no pay is due,
Seeing the beer is a worthless brew,
Muddy of color and flat and sour,
Drawn from the vat in an evil hour.
Further, he claimeth of startled Jan
Gold for redress of his inner man.

[91]

What did the worshipful Schepens do?
Think you they summoned a learnèd crew
Laden with volumes, retorts, and vials
Such as bewilder our modern trials?
Nothing of ptomaines nor germs knew they;
Naught of the microbe that stalks by day;
Nothing they knew of those wondrous men
Skilled in the slights of the subtle pen.
Nothing they knew of our modern shame—
Perjury sanctioned by Learning's name.
The highway to Justice was broad and clear:
"Court is adjourned to inspect the beer."

Out to the open the jury wan
With doubtful Jacobus and hopeful Jan.
Nothing was heard for an hour or twain
But mellow gurgles, the soft refrain
Of deep-drawn breathing and smack of zest
That tell of the spirit of man at rest,
While the jury, seated along a fence,
Absorbed and digested the evidence.

Seemly the session, though all too short
E'en for the litigants. Soon the Court
Gravely convened at its former stand,
Wiping its mouth on the back of its hand,
And spake with conviction, as jurors should:
"Verdict for plaintiff. Said beer was good."

ON THE HARLEM

The hand that ruled the helm was yours,
* The arm that bent the oar was mine;*
The breeze that blew across the moors
* Was breath of meadows blent with brine;*

It whirled the reddened leaf along,
* It stirred your silken-tendriled hair,*
It teased the wave to rill in song,
* It played upon my shoulders bare.*

In time with even dip and swing
* And crisp of feathered oars aslant,*
We roused the crags where laurels cling
* With Eton's mellow rowing-chant.*

So down that sparkling reach we came
  On keel of cedar, silver-shod,
Our bows aglow with leaves aflame
  And gunwale-deep in goldenrod.

WILLIAM THE TESTY

WILHELMUS KIEFT is generally admitted to have been the worst of the Dutch governors of New York; and, even waiving his minor faults and offenses, he undoubtedly deserves that bad eminence because of his cruelty and perfidy which brought upon the settlement the most terrible of the Indian wars that hampered its growth. Still it is to be remembered in his favor that he maintained the city's basic traditions of tolerance and hospitality by welcoming fugitives from religious bigotry, such as Lady Deborah Moody, from less liberal New England; and also it is well to bear in mind that Washington Irving's lively caricature of the peppery little Director in his brimstone breeches was actually a satire on Thomas

Jefferson. For fear that I may be accused of following too closely in Irving's footsteps by likewise applying the past to the immediate present, I must plead that the following ballad was written and printed in the year 1900.

WILLIAM THE TESTY

AFAR in the ages of quaint renown
There ruled o'er the germ of this mighty town
A potentate, famed for a wondrous knack
Of breeding dissension and brewing wrack.
Oh, he was a tart little pepper-pot!
A simmering kettle, forever hot!
A hedgehog abristle with puissant ire,
A little volcano of smothered fire;
Forever intruding a muddling hand
In matters beyond him to understand,
Upsetting the work of a dozen men
And fuming and fussing enough for ten.
A meddlesome, quarrelsome, peevish sprite,
He bustled and bickered from dawn till night.
He troubled his folk with a hundred griefs:
He kindled the rage of the savage chiefs,
And tomahawk, arrow, and brand came down
Through desolate fields to a mourning town.

Though skilled in the practice of wordy strife
And cursed with a tongue like a poisoned knife,

He fronted a foeman of like degree
When he blundered afoul of the Dominie.
For Parson Bogardus, the stern and leal,
Was deeply concerned for the public weal,
And loudly he thundered in strong dispraise,
Denouncing the governor's evil ways.
"The preacher's a sot!" came the fierce retort;
"His sermons are stupid and none too short!"
Small wonder, forsooth, that the parson dinned
His wrath from the pulpit: "Ach! Duyvil's kind!
Defamer of righteousness!" then a roar—
"My goats are as good as the governor!"
The magistrate's vengeance was swift and fell;
He marshaled his troops at the stroke of bell,
And vainly the Dominie strove to cheer
The sinning and sorrowful; every ear
With drum-roll and trumpet and martial sound
Was filled, and the sermon was wholly drowned!

The burghers, aghast at the wild debate
And utter disruption of Church and state,
Deported the disputants out of hand
To settle their feud in the fatherland.
The governor burdened the vessel's hold
With marvelous treasure of goblin gold

8   [99]

Achieved under starlight and lantern-glow
In the mystical mines of the Ramapo.
Thus laden, the vessel was tempest tossed,
And parson and governor both were lost!
Yet—there is a legend in hut and hall
That Governor Kieft wasn't drowned at all!
But, spirited off with his fairy gold,
He drowses and dreams in a mountain hold
Like Arthur, or Ogier the lordly Dane,
Some day to return to his own domain.

And now when a bickering breaks the gloom
And wakens old ghosts in the mayor's room,
When portly commissioners dread the ban
That darts from the orbs of a mighty man,
When frightened attendants stand quaking by
And browbeat petitioners turn and fly,
Methinks he hath come to his home once more—
The stanch little burgh on the Hudson's shore;
'Tis William the Testy, no modern sham,
That governs the town of New Amsterdam!

THE ROAD

My way of life is a winding road,
  A road that wanders, yet turns not back,
Where one should go with as light a load
  As well may be in a traveler's pack;

A road that rambles through marsh and wood,
  Meadow and waste, to the cloudy end;
But, smooth or rugged, I find it good,
  For something's always around the bend.

There may be storms in the bleak defiles,
  But oh, the calm of the valley's breast!
There may be toil on the upward miles,
  But oh, the joy of the mountain-crest!

And here's a thistle and there's a rose,
  And next—whatever the road may send;
For onward ribbons the way I chose,
  With something always around the bend.

Then come and travel my road with me
    Through windy passes or waves of flowers!
Though long and weary the march may be,
    The rover's blessing shall still be ours:

"A noonday halt at a crystal well,
    A word and smile with a passing friend,
A song to sing and a tale to tell,
    And something coming around the bend!'"

THE PIRATE'S SPUKE

IN 1612 Captain Adrian Block established a trading-post on the island of Manhattan, and two years later, in the *Onrust* or *Restless*, a stout craft of native pine, the first ship ever launched in the waters of New York, he set forth on his memorable voyage of exploration along the eastern shore of the island into the unknown Sound. On the figurative map of his expedition that he caused to be made, "Hellegatt" appears as the name of the arm of the sea that we now call the East River; and it is evident that the patriotic captain named the strait in honor of "De Helle-gatt," that is, "the bright or beautiful pass," a stream that flows into the West Schelde through the southern part of his own province of Zeeland, that nurse of hardy sailors. But after sundry Dutch skippers had met with trouble and disaster among the rocks, whirlpools, and currents off Hallet's Point, they testily changed the name to "Hel-gatt," or, as we make it, "Hell Gate," confining the application of that ominous title to the region of danger.

Now it is notorious that the devil never declines an invitation, and from that moment the passage became a veritable picnic-ground for all the imps; and its rocks—the Hog's Back, the Hen and Chickens, the Frying-pan and the Pot—were the scene of many an infernal revel until the spirits of

evil were exorcised by the potent charm of dynamite in 1876.

The identity of a dreadful apparition, the pirate's spuke, or ghost, that haunted Hell Gate until shot with a silver bullet by Governor Peter Stuyvesant, has long been a matter of dispute. The infant colony of New Amsterdam was visited by many pirates, such as Captain Sebastian de Raeff, and doubtless some of these perished in the wild tide-rush of the East River in their attempts to reach the town through the treacherous channel. Perhaps the ghost was that of Captain de Raeff himself, perhaps it was that of his lieutenant, Jan van Campen; perhaps—but the secret is lost beneath the foam of Hell Gate.

THE PIRATE'S SPUKE

᛫LEAVE the dull present, to seek awhile
The little Dutch burgh on Manhattan Isle
Under that ruler of adamant,
Sturdy old Governor Stuyvesant.
Here is a circle of broad-backed men
Harking, while Trumpeter Pietersen
Opens a budget of wondrous lore
Of the deeds of the doughty old governor;
Sings him triumphant o'er man and elf;
Yea (whisper low!), o'er the Duyvil himself!

In the rock-toothed strait where the three tides meet
    Ye may cast your lines at will
While the sun is high in an honest sky
    And the ravening wave is still;

But 'ware the reefs! under midnight's roof
    When the roaring eddies swell!
For the rocks are marked with the cloven hoof
    And the smut of the brands of hell.

Like a slavered wolf the torrent moans
    And raves through deeps and shoals;
The air is filled with the warning groans
    And wails of perished souls;

And the Duyvil squats on the Hog's Back high
    When the angry cloud-banks form,
And his fiddle squalls to the murky sky
    In hail of the brewing storm.

So he snareth fish for his grimy clan,
    And the foaming brine brawls hot
As he griddles his prey on the Frying-pan
    Or seethes it in the Pot!

All day a sun of sullen red
    Through mists had glowered down;
That night 'twas inky black o'erhead
    And a wild wind smote the town.

The March sky broke with a crashing roar,
    But never a raindrop fell;
And a dreadful laugh shook the eastern shore—
    The mirthless laugh of hell!

There, in the curd of the churning vat
  Where naught of earth could float,
A black-faced, scar-browed seaman sat
  In the stern of a tossing boat.

He wore a scarf at his evil throat,
  And the hat of a picaroon,
And every boss of his blue sea-coat
  Was a shining gold doubloon.

His belt of net with pistolet
  And burnished dirk was hung;
The thunder's growl and tempest's howl
  Waxed louder as he sung:

"Oh, golden Main and fleets of Spain!
  No more my chests ye fill,
For here I stay till Judgment Day
  To work my Master's will!"

Out stumped our stanch old governor,
  A musket in his hand:
"Now get thee gone, thou devil's spawn,
  Nor longer vex my land!"

"Oh, I may not go and I will not go,"
  That girding goblin cried,
"While the trade-winds blow and the salt waves
  flow
  And the white moon rules the tide."

"Thou wretched fry! wouldst thou defy
  My will with tawdry spell?
Thou thing unclean, thou ghoul obscene,
  Hence! hie thee back to hell!"

"Oh, silver and gold, and silver and gold!
  Rich, rich my Master's fee!
So here I ride, whate'er betide,
  Until he looseth me."

The governor raised his musket true
  And aimed through spume and brine:
"Dost silver crave, thou losel knave?
  Then take this gift of mine!"

The bullet was cast of the silver bright;
  'Twas blessed by the Dominie
With a mystic word—and it smote that sprite
  In the place where a heart should be.

A DEAL IN REAL ESTATE

WHILE the early history of the colonies on Manhattan was stained by several cruel Indian wars, the relations between the Dutch settlers and the aborigines were generally not unpleasant, and, despite the fact that the pale-face had an uncomfortable habit of getting the best of the bargain, there are many instances of warm friendships between red and white.

A DEAL IN REAL ESTATE

BARENDT CUYLER, Indian trader,
   Shrewd, but honest as the light,
Merry-hearted, wise, and witty,
   Loved alike by red and white,

Sat and pondered in the sunshine,
   Puffing at his pipe the while,
Where the brawling Spuyten Duyvil
   Foams on Mannahatta's Isle.

Arrow-swift, a birchen vessel
   Shot across the winding creek;
Up the bank strode Wetamoset,
   Sachem of the Weckquaesgeek.

"Hail!" the Dutchman called in greeting.
   "Hail!" the crested chief replied,
Gracious as a king in exile.
   Pipe to pipe and side by side,

Long they smoked in friendly silence,
   Gazing on the rapid stream,
Till the chieftain softly murmured,
   "Wetamoset dreamed a dream."

"Tell thy dream." Then quoth the sachem,
   Guileless as a babe new-born,
"Wetamoset dreamed his brother
   Gave him gun and powder-horn."

Grave and silent, Barendt Cuyler
   Sought his cabin's open door,
Filled a horn with large-grained powder,
   Chose a musket from his store,

Gave them to the stolid chieftain,
   Who, with courteous ado,
Bearing off the light-won plunder
   Launched again his light canoe.

———

Wetamoset, sage and war-chief,
   Stood before his lodge at morn;
Dark behind him rose his woodland,
   Green before him waved his corn.

Mosholu to Spuyten Duyvil
  Poured a rill of liquid light;
Up the slope came Barendt Cuyler,
  Loved alike by red and white.

Full and friendly was his welcome,
  Long he tarried there, to speak
Pleasant words of kindly counsel
  For the folk of Weckquaesgeek.

Then, beneath his eyebrow's shadow
  Flashed and danced a mirthful gleam;
Spoke the trader: "Wetamoset,
  Barendt Cuyler dreamed a dream."

"Let him tell it." Then the trader:
  "Cuyler, sleeping by the lin,
Dreamed that Wetamoset gave him
  All of Papparinamin!"

Ruefully the stately sachem
  Viewed the province of that dream,
All the pleasant island-meadow
  'Twixt the marshland and the stream.

9

Arm in air, he traced the boundary,
Wooded height and reedy shore:
"All that land is thine, my brother.
Brother—let us dream no more!"

POSSESSION

When soft I lay in the mossy bed
  That swells to the foot of the hemlock-tree,
In the pride of a lover's heart I said,
  "The sweet, green woods belong to me!"

But the woodchuck gray and the brown-eyed doe
  And the chipmunk, rocked on the hazel stem,
And the hare and the deermouse answered, "No!"—
  The sweet, green woods belonged to them!

Then the jack-in-the-pulpits, friends of youth,
  Looked archly out from their purpling hoods
With an elfin laugh as they told the truth:
  "We all belong to the sweet, green woods!"

AT the extreme northwestern end of the island
of Manhattan, bordered by the broad Hudson
and the curving Spuyten Duyvil, rises the promontory that a few still call by its ancient name of
Cock Hill or Cox's Hill, an untamed region of
cliff, ravine, and woodland. Probably from this
eminence as well as from the fortified height of
Nipnichsen on the Westchester shore across the
creek, the Indians of the island first sounded in
European ears their fierce war-cry, "Hoach, hoach,
ha, ha, hach, woach!" as they shot their arrows
and hurled their lances at Henry Hudson's vessel.
This is a place brimming over with magic—upper,
lower, and middle magic. A deep glade, known as
The Clove, leads through woods to a little patch
of meadow backed by lofty cliffs and opening out
upon the Spuyten Duyvil. Here a spring of the
purest water flows into the creek, while above it
grows a great tulip-tree, by far the largest tree
on the island. In a haunted cave still to be seen

under the eastward shadow of the cliffs there once dwelt an ancient Indian medicine-man, hight Moaqua. A kindly old wizard, his counsel was much sought by the rosy maidens of New Haarlem and New Amsterdam on all subjects from matters of the dairy even unto matters of the heart; and before he vanished from mortal eyes in the mysterious manner characteristic of all true wizards, he imparted some of his mystic power to the beautiful spring near his dwelling-place, ever after known as the Wizard's Well.

WIZARD'S WELL

"Trudchen! Trudchen!" teased the maids,
  Laughed the lads of gallant mien;
"Leave your gloomy forest glades!
  Join our dance upon the green!"

Trudchen never turned her head;
  Light as wind-blown thistledown
Up the woodland path she sped
  Far above the step-roofed town.

"Trudchen! Trudchen!" sang the birds,
  Called the squirrels, high in air;
"Here are lilies, white as curds,
  Velvet moss and maidenhair.

"Stay with us, oh, Sweet, Sweet, Sweet!
  Play with us, and fear no harm!"
Onward flew her constant feet;
  Pause or word had broke the charm.

[120]

*Light as wind-blown thistle down
Up the woodland path she sped.*

Soon beside the pool she stood,
  Underneath the cliff-walled hill
Shadowed by the ancient wood
  Bordered by the sparkling kill;

Bending low, with coral mouth
  Sipped the waters of the well;
Closed her eyes and faced the south;
  Wished her wish and spoke the spell:

"Wizard chief, whose haunted cave
  Hides where mountain-laurels cling;
Red Moaqua, thou that gave
  Secret gifts to bless thy spring,

"Hear the words my grandam taught!
  Hear the unforgotten spell!
Own the charm thy magic wrought!
  Grant the wish I may not tell!"

Steered where Spuyten Duyvil Kill
  Drinks of Hudson's ample flow,
Driven with a lusty will
  Landward rode the broad bateau.

Rich in peltries, plain and pied,
  Spoil of beaver, mink, and deer,
Marten fur and panther hide,
  Gaily came the pioneer.

Home! from wilds and craggy caves,
  Lairs of beasts and savage men.
"Trudchen! Trudchen!" lisped the waves;
  "*We* have brought him home again!"

Light o'er rock and fallen bole
  Leaped the youth in glad surprise;
Soft behind the girl he stole,
  Gently kissed the hooded eyes.

Tulip-tree, whose mighty shade
  Gives the well a deeper hue,
Tell the wish that Trudchen made!
  Tell me—did that wish come true?

HALLOWE'EN CHARM

Fern seed, hemp seed, water of the well,
  Bark of wizard hazel-wand, berry of the bay,
Let the fairy gifts of you mingle with the spell,
  Guard the precious life and soul of him that's far
    away!

Oak slip, thorn slip, crystal of the dew,
  Morsel of his native earth, shoot of mountain pine,
Lend his arm the strength of you, let his eye be true,
  Send him like the thunderbolt to break the foeman's
    line!

Rose leaf, elm leaf, kernel of the wheat,
  Airy waft of thistledown, feather of the wren,
Bring him peace and happiness, let his dream be
    sweet,
  Take my secret thought to him and call him home
    again!

BORGER JORIS'S HAMMER

EARLY in the history of New Amsterdam Borger Joris, the smith, set up his forge on the Strand of the East River just below the palisades of Wall Street, where Hanover Square is to-day. Hearty, patriotic, and pugnacious, he was the last man to stand by Governor Stuyvesant in his defiance of the English fleet, and left the city in disgust after the surrender. The scene of his youthful adventure, narrated in the following ballad, the Glen of the Little Gray Men, is part of the glade of the wooded Clove at Spuyten Duyvil.

BORGER JORIS'S HAMMER

A LANDHOLDING freeman, a burgher of pith,
Is big Borger Joris, New Amsterdam's smith.
Just south of the Wall where the ferryboat swings,
His forge-fire blazes; his sledge-hammer rings
On plowshare, on coulter, on scythe, ax, and bill.
He beats the white iron that shapes to his will.
Thrice hard were the labors of forest and farm
If gone were the skill of that muscular arm.

The coals of the smithy to ashes have burned;
The daylight is ebbing; in leisure well earned
The smith's at the doorway, his face to the breeze
That blows from the harbor. Young Peter De
    Vries,
His curly-haired 'prentice, as eager for play
And chary of work as a boy of to-day—
Who lounges full-length on the turf at his side,
Heaves up the great hammer, stout Joris's pride,
And queries, "Good master, now tell me, I pray:
You've wrought on the anvil for many a day

Scythe, horseshoe, and anchor, the great and the
  small,
But who forged the hammer that forges them all?"

A huge, kindly hand like the paw of a bear
Is lost in the youth's tumbled masses of hair
As Joris makes answer: "That hammer was new
When I was a worthless apprentice like you.
But fill me a pipe and a tankard of ale,
My lad, and I'll tell you its wonderful tale.

"In fall when the maples were tinging with red,
When goldenrod waved, and the azure o'erhead
Was mellow with haze, like a slip-halter colt
I scampered free-footed through meadow and
  holt,
A truant; far better the fowl-haunted sedge
I loved than the anvil, the bellows, and sledge.

"Well north, on the sweep of the eddying kill
That limits our island, arises a hill,
A deep-fissured foreland of green-wooded glades
Where chestnuts are gathered by Indian maids
And cress in the summer. So mild is the air
That columbines bloom at the earliest there,

[128]

And bobolink chirrups his mellowest staves.
Oh, green are its laurels and mossy its caves
And clear are its wells—may they never run
      dry!—
You rascal! you know the spot better than I.

"'Twas there that I loitered, too happy for words,
To chaff with the squirrels, to chirp to the
      birds,
To wander, high-souled and adventurous, fain
To search every nook of my lovely domain;
Then, stretched in the shade of a great tree that
      grows
Cliff-sheltered, spring-watered, I lay in a doze
To dream out my day-dream; when, ringing and
      clear,
The clink of a forge-hammer smote on my ear,
Sore blow to my conscience! I sprang to my
      feet
And marveled and trembled; it *must* be a cheat!
Yet, no; I saw clearly: The nave of the glen
Was filled with an army of little gray men
Not three feet in stature! They swarmed on the
      crags,
Their tasseled caps waving like little red flags,

Their buskined feet twinkling, their beards flowing
    free,
Their eyes in a riot of mischievous glee

"And this wore a jerkin and that wore a
    smock.
Some tended a blaze in a cup-shapen rock;
Some wheeled the black ore from the earth where
    it bides
To smelt out the iron; yet others, besides,
Made ready wee anvils, or heated thick wedges
Of metal to whiteness. Then, down came the
    sledges,
And up flew the sparkles! Oh, wonders they
    wrought
In well-tempered iron, and swifter than thought.
And never a gnome of them boggled or shirked,
And ever the Little Men sang as they worked:

"'Clang! cling! the hammers swing,
The flame-tongues leap, the anvils ring!
Commingling strength and craft and zeal
In welded bar and tempered steel
We frame our work with chanted spell
And cool it in the Wizard's Well.

"'Ho! ho! the bellows blow,
The coals awake, the forges glow!
Then let cold iron drink of fire
And weld the sledge that shall not tire,
The ax to lay the forest low,
The share to plow, the scythe to mow!

" 'Hiss! hiss! the waters kiss
The finished tools, and naught's amiss.
Now stamp on each the elfin brand
That none shall ever fail the hand
In meadow, forest, forge, or mill,
That works with craft and might and will!'

"A gnome with a frown and a gnome with a smile
(Like Warning and Blessing) advanced; from the
      pile
A fire-new hammer, with handle complete,
They carried, and silently placed at my feet.
I gripped on the gift with a venturesome fist
And—puff!—all the pageantry passed like a mist!

"So, back from the wildwood, more earnest and
      strong,
I bore to the smithy the hammer and song.

10   [131]

And oft as I labor I think of the glen
And echo the chant of the Little Gray Men.
And still do I mark with their magical brand
Each scythe, ax, and plowshare that comes from
my hand
To bless with the succor of elf-given skill
The mortals who wield them with power and will."

A LILT IN FALL

The brown of her eyes in the oaken leaf,
  The stir of her sighs in the mountain fir,
The scent of her breath in the garnered sheaf—
  Oh, all the world shall sing of her!

THE CHANGE OF FLAGS

IN August, 1664, while there was yet peace between Holland and Great Britain, Colonel Nichols sailed up the Bay and demanded the surrender of New Amsterdam. The demand was backed by a show of four war-ships with a hundred guns and a full complement of sailors, a body of five hundred regular troops, and a considerable force of New-Englanders, Long Island settlers, and Indians. The fort was dilapidated, was commanded by the hills to the northward, and Stuyvesant had at his service but two hundred and fifty soldiers; yet he obstinately refused to yield, replying in simple faith to the English commander:

As touching the threats in your conclusion, we have nothing to answer, only that we fear nothing but what God (who is just as merciful) shall lay upon us, all things being in His gracious disposal; and we may as well be preserved by Him with small forces as by a great army; which makes us wish you all happiness and prosperity, and recommend *you* to His protection.

My lords,

Your thrice humble and affectionate servant and friend,

P. STUYVESANT.

But resistance was too clearly hopeless. The clamors of the people and the entreaties of his most trusted counselors at last won from the governor a reluctant consent to the articles of capitulation, and the Dominie fairly dragged him from the bastions of the fort, protesting, "I had much rather be carried out dead!"

Yet some there were, headed by Borger Joris, the sturdy blacksmith, who, refusing to accept English rule, withdrew in disgust into the remote interior; whence their stalwart descendants returned to do yeoman service against their traditional foes in the Revolutionary War.

On the other hand, it is pleasant to remember that the doughty governor spent the last years of his long life in the city that he had ruled most ably, if somewhat imperiously, mellowing with age and loved and respected alike by Dutch and English; and that his bones still rest in the vault of old St. Mark's Church, within the soil of his cherished island.

THE CHANGE OF FLAGS

A FLURRIED scud of sunlit sails
  To make the sheltered port;
A flash of steel, a trumpet-peal
  Within the seaward fort;
The grave-browed burgomasters
  Have sought the council-hall;
Van Dyck has raised the yeomanry
  To man the northern wall;
The Watch is up with ancient arms
  That foiled the steel of Spain,
And groups of anxious burghers
  Are clustered on The Plain.

And here is Abram Pietersen,
  And hither from The Strand
Comes stalwart Borger Joris,
  His hammer in his hand.
The vrouws have left their bread to burn,
  The children leave their play—
"The Englishmen! the Englishmen!
  Their ships are in the Bay!"

The stubborn Heer Direktor
    Upon the rampart's height
Roused up his keen-eyed gunners,
    Their linstocks blazing bright:
"Now make your weapons ready,
And hold your courage high!
(I'll hear the cannon's music
    Once more before I die!)
And show these haughty English
    That ye are of the strain
That held the walls of Leyden
    Against the might of Spain!"

A hand upon his shoulder
    And Peter turned in pride;
The Dominie, his comrade,
    Was standing at his side.
"Old friend, and trusty soldier,"
    That man of God began,
"I know thy heart of courage
    That fears not any man;
Yet save thy helpless city!
    Provoke not ruthless war!
Alone, surrounded, friendless,
    Outnumbered as we are.

[137]

Our sires held leagured Leyden
  By spear and carronade;
But faithful Father William
  Had sworn to bear them aid.
But spare a helpless people,
  Beset on every hand,
Divorced by leagues of ocean
  From home and fatherland!"

Then paused the stern Direktor,
  While through a dimming mist
He viewed his little city
  He clenched his iron fist
And smote the useless cannon.
  "Thou speakest truth!" he said;
"I yield!—but, God in heaven!
  I would that I were dead!"

Then, shoulder touching shoulder,
  With drum and trumpet-peal,
The princely flag of Orange
  Above their caps of steel,
The city's stanch defenders
  Marched shoreward, unashamed;
And, red against the heavens
  The flag of England flamed.

[138]

An angry man was Joris
  Beside the blazing forge
To see above the rampart
  The banner of St. George!
"So! must we swear allegiance
  And bow our necks?" quoth he,
"And pay our tithes to puppets
  Of kings beyond the sea?
What boot to fashion plowshares
  And scythes, but hapless toil!
Oh, had I beaten broadswords
  Ye might have held your soil!

"Ho! freemen! leave the city
  For dukes to make or mar!
We'll raise our rugged hamlets
  Among the hills afar;
And there I'll hammer sabers
  For better men to use;
We'll breed a race of soldiers!
  A race with hearts and thews!
Our children's children's children
  Perchance may live to fling
Away these galling shackles
  And scorn the tyrant king;

And when they've struck for freedom,
    And when our debt is paid,
They'll think on Borger Joris
    That wrought the battle-blade!"

English
Colonial
Period

POLLY CORTELYOU

THE little English fleet that in August, 1664, sailed into the harbor with the forces under Col. Richard Nichols, brought in its wake, besides a change in government, the beginnings of many other changes, social as well as political. There was, it is true, a brief reversal to the old order when a Dutch fleet retook the city from the invaders. But by a treaty that ended an indecisive war, New Amsterdam became permanently New York; old Dutch customs slowly yielded to livelier English fashions; the English element grew preponderant with the rapid increase of population, and the little town became more and more a city. But for many years New York presented a strange contrast of nationalities and an often comical blending of city and country scenes and manners. The following little social incident occurred in the early years of the new régime.

POLLY CORTELYOU

"Pretty Polly Cortelyou,
　Mistress of the dairy,
Born a dainty little shrew,
　Sprightly and contrary,

"Sweet of manner, neat in
　　dress,
　Buxom little charmer;
Who would have such love-
　liness
　Wasted on a farmer!"

Built when only moor and wood
　Edged the rustic byway,
Now her father's bouwerie stood
　Fronting on the highway

Where, in silken revelry,
　Plumes and powdered tresses,
Passed Manhattan's chivalry,
　Swept their hearts' princèsses.

[144]

Rosy Polly Cortelyou
  Kept the dasher turning,
Panting as the butter grew
  Stiffer with her churning;

Frowning still on Harry Gray,
  Merry spark of fashion,
Sipping buttermilk and whey
  Just to cool his passion.

"Go!" said she, "thou face of brass;
  Save thy coat of scarlet!
How should e'er a farmer lass
  Wed a lazy varlet!"

"Cruel Polly! leave the churn!
  Think me not a rake, dear.
Sure," the gallant said, "I'd turn
  Shepherd for your sake, dear.

"Nay, you doubt me? Can you ask
  Proof I love you madly?
Set me any servile task;
  Faith, I'll do it gladly."

[145]

"Wilt thou then," the maiden spoke,
  "Bear, till I enlarge thee,
Milking-pails and dairy yoke
  Wheresoe'er I charge thee?"

"Sweet, I'd bear them," vowed the youth,
  "Just to do thy pleasure,
Clear to Spain!—and back, forsooth,
  Heaping full of treasure."

Round his neck the dimpling miss
  Bound the yoke, to tame him.
(If he tried to snatch a kiss,
  Truly, do you blame him?)

Laughing at his helpless plight,
  Led him from the dairy
(So a Jack-o'-lantern sprite,
  So an antic fairy,

Threading bog or muddy shore,
  Draws a luckless mortal),
Through the house, towàrd the door,
  Opened wide the portal.

[146]

Then, that wicked little cheat,
  Laughing still, to blind him,
Thrust him headlong to the street,
  Snapped the lock behind him.

All Manhattan's brave array
  Stopped and stared in wonder.
All Manhattan's gallants gay
  Split their sides asunder.

There he stood in silken coat,
  Rapier silver-hilted,
Snowy scarf about his throat,
  Beaver bravely tilted,

Harry Gray, the ballroom's pride,
  Yoke across his shoulders,
Brimming pails on either side,
  Joy of all beholders.

Heartless Polly shrieked with mirth,
  Screened behind the casement.
Open! open! kindly earth!
  Cover his abasement!

Each of twenty youths, they say,
  Solemn as a major,
Took his oath that Harry Gray
  Did it on a wager.

Eight-and-forty ladies fair
  (Can a man deceive them?)
Dropped their eyes and heard them swear—
  Didn't quite believe them.

Gallants, heed! 'Twere well ye should,
  Be they ne'er so loving,
Chain your hearts; to field and wood
  Send them not a-roving.

Woman-craft in subtle toys
  All your wit surpasses.
Let the canny country boys
  Woo the farmer lasses!

CITY HALL PARK

Ere Cabot's prow was westward turned,
  Before old Hudson came,
Upon this island acre burned
  The Red Man's council flame.

Then here the settler's cattle grazed
  Along the bowered track;
And here his bell-mouthed musket blazed
  And drove the savage back.

But yonder rose the gallows-tree
  Where, calm and fearless-eyed,
Our first sad pledge to Liberty,
  Great-hearted Leisler died.

And hither flocked from shops and farms,
  When Freedom's summons flew,
Those large-boned, sun-browned men-at-arms
  That wore the buff and blue.

[149]

Oh, build your walls, for build you will,
  On earth less dearly known;
Leave this one spot unburdened still
  With tyrant steel and stone!—

A scroll whereon brave youth shall trace
  Brave deeds of days gone by,
A shrine, a little, hallowed space
  Unroofed beneath the sky.

THE STORM SHIP

IN early English colonial times, especially in Col. Benjamin Fletcher's administration from 1692 to 1698, the city of New York was a veritable paradise of pirates, who carried thither for sale the spoil of the Indian seas and swaggered boldly in the streets, having, it is pretty well established, purchased protection, if not from the governor himself, at least from his trusted advisers. Naturally the outfitting of buccaneering vessels and the marketing of the treasure that they brought into port were wonderfully good for business, wherefore great was the righteous indignation of the honorable merchants of the city when Fletcher's successor, the inflexible Earl of Bellomont, presumed to interfere with the profitable traffic and strove to bring the pirates to justice.

Everybody has heard of Capt. William Kidd, once a respectable householder of Liberty Street; how, in 1696, empowered with King William's commission, he sailed in the *Adventure* galley to prey upon the pirates of the Indian Ocean; how he turned pirate himself, and how punishment overtook him. It is known that before Kidd surrendered himself to justice he sailed up Long Island Sound as far as Oyster Bay and left part of his booty at Gardiner's Island, whence it was recovered by the government; but all wise men of the sea agree that the fate of his piratical vessel or vessels and the hiding-places of his fabulous treasures remain dark and delightful mysteries.

Vague stories of the terrible captain still echo among the Highlands of the Hudson, where Caldwell's Landing bears the alternative name of "Kidd's Point," and where "Kidd's Plug Cliff" is still shown as a repository of his golden hoard; moreover, there is a well-attested tradition that the charred hulk of his hapless ship still lies beneath the waters of the river at the foot of Dunderberg.

THE STORM SHIP

HER sails are wove of the fogs that flee;
  Her masts are wraiths of the Baltic firs;
The phosphor-glow of a sultry sea
  Is the only foam that her forefoot stirs.

Her lanterns gleam with the wan corpse-light,
  The clouds roll black where her helmsman steers;
The silent shapes on her main-deck's height
  Are of Hudson old and his mutineers.

She comes from the capes of Labrador;
  Through the death-white fleet of the North she
      glides,
And the fisher-craft of the mist-hung shore
  Keep close in port when the Storm Ship rides.

Full-crammed with Eastern silk and gold—
  A guilty treasure, won amid
Red wrack and slaughter—homeward rolled
  The pirate craft of Captain Kidd.

And, "Westward, ho!" the chorus rang;
  "Our hatches brim with precious store.
Let beggars fight and cowards hang!
  But we shall live like lords, ashore."

"A sail to windward; ho! a sail!"
  The lookout from the foretop cried.
The captain heard that boding hail;
  He gripped the cutlass at his side.

"She comes in chase—no flag displayed;
  Belike a war-ship of the Crown—
Run out the starboard carronade
  And send her mainmast toppling down!"

The gunner aimed—and well he could;
  The linstock blazed, the chain-shot flew;
It brought no crash of rending wood,
  Yet cut the mainmast through and through.

It cut the mast before their eyes,
　Yet mast and spars stood stiff and strong;
And underneath the darkening skies
　That drumly vessel bowled along,

No murmur in her bellied clouds
　Of canvas, gray without a fleck;
The breeze was voiceless in her shrouds,
　The crew stood silent on her deck;

And, like a red-hot cannon-ball,
　The sullen sun in skies of lead
Revealed, beneath a murky pall,
　The livid faces of the dead!

Round spun the wheel! In panic, blind
　To all but that dread shape abeam,
They fled, a rising gale behind,
　Up Hudson's glamour-haunted stream.

Proud Mannahatta's island key
　Was left astern. The sun went down.
They swept the shores of Tappan Zee
　Beneath the heights of Tarrytown.

They drove across the sea-broad sweep
   That laps the hills of Haverstraw
To Dunderberg's enchanted steep
   Whose goblins keep the vale in awe.

Around the frowning mountain boiled
   That swirling ebb, the Devil's Race;
In vain the tide-held pirate toiled!
   While onward drove the wraith in chase.

New horror froze the cutthroat band;
   For, as the phantom closer came,
Her ghostly captain waved his hand—
   And Dunderberg was ringed with flame!

Red levin smote the buccaneer;
   Her kindled rigging lit the night;
And helter-skelter, mad with fear,
   The pirates plunged in headlong flight.

The crackling flame-tongues searched the hold;
   A rending crash, a wild turmoil
Of smoke and foam—and Hudson rolled
   Above a wealth of blood-won spoil.

And he that 'scaped the flame and wave
   Was spared to sound the depths of shame;
For him a dungeon's living grave,
   A felon's death, a blackened name.

.   .   .   .   .   .

Her sails are wove of the fogs that flee;
   Her masts are wraiths of the Baltic firs;
The phosphor-glow of a sultry sea
   Is the only foam that her forefoot stirs.

When she lays her head to the whooping gale
 And the corpse-light flares on her lofty sides,
Oh, it's run for port with a thrice-reefed sail!
 For the waves wax rich where the Storm Ship
  rides.

THE THANK-OFFERING

OVERBECK, the Forest Preacher,
  Bent his silvered head:
"Harvest yields for every creature
  Food in store," he said.

"Ye that know your Lord is living,
  Witnessing His grace,
Heap your tithes of all His giving
  Round His altar-place."

Ere November breezes blowing
  Bared the silver birch,
Harvest-plenty overflowing
  Filled the little church.

Farmer-folk in pleasant parley
  Praised the crops they'd reared—
Dirck Van Brunt his sheaves of barley
  Yellow as his beard,

Peter Smit his orchard's bounty;
  Boastful Gert Von Horn
Swore no croft in all the county
  Equaled his for corn.

Housewives showed in oaken caskets
  Butter firm and good.
Children brought in birchen baskets
  Nuts of copse and wood.

All was set before the altar,
  When across the moor
Crept the widow, Gretel Balter,
  Wrinkled, bent, and poor.

"She! that earns with all her labors
  Scant enough to live,
Helped and clothed by kindly neighbors—
  What hath *she* to give?"

"Come, behold the widow's treasure!"
  All the world drew near.
Just a little earthen measure
  Filled with water clear.

Just an earthen cruse, upon it
  Writ in letters plain—
Yea, and all her world might con it—
  "God be thanked for rain."

Overbeck, the Forest Preacher,
  Raised his noble head:
"She, not I, shall be your teacher,
  Oh, my friends," he said.

"What are treasures proudly tendered?
  Dross before His throne!
Humble offerings, humbly rendered,
  Loveth God, alone."

12

SAXON HARVEST HEALTH

Here's to the plow that furrowed,
Here's to the hand that sowed,
Here's to the rake that harrowed,
Here's to the arm that mowed!

Blest with the choice of blessings
Are orchard and hill and plain—
The blessing of Grapes and Apples,
The blessing of Sheaves of Grain.

TUBBY HOOK

ABOUT two-thirds of a mile below Spuyten Duyvil, at the old settlement of Inwood from where the Fort Lee ferry carries picnic-parties across the Hudson to the Palisades, there is a rock-edged cape which, before filling-in operations changed its rounded outline, by its appearance alone justified its old Dutch name of "Tobbe Hoeck"—the Cape of the Tub—now rendered "Tubby Hook."

After much inquiry I finally learned from the bearded lips of an old settler the true explanation of this promising name. And as the memory of the narrator extends back to the time "when Canal Street was 'way down to the Battery," his authority on legendary matters is plainly indisputable.

TUBBY HOOK

Mevrouw von Weber was brisk thôugh fat;
She loved her neighbor, she loved her cat,
She loved her husband; but, here's the rub—
Beyond all conscience she loved her tub!
She rubbed and scrubbed with strange delight,
She scrubbed and rubbed from morn till night;
    Her earthly hope
    Was placed in soap;
Her walls and chimneypiece fairly shone,
Her skirts were starched so they stood alone!

By mop and duster and broom she swore.
    She scrubbed the floor
    Until she wore
The oak in channels from door to door.
The flood she reveled in never ebbed,
    And hill to dale
    Retold the tale
That both her hands and her feet were webbed!

Now Hans, her husband, was mild and meek;
He let her scrub through the livelong week;
But when the sud of her washtub churned
On Easter Sunday!—the earthworm turned.
    "Nay, vrouw," quoth he,
    "Let labor be!
This day when all of the world's at feast
Thou'lt wash no more—in *my* house, at least!"
She stopped her toil at her lord's command.
    Without a sound
    She flaunted round
And took her tub to the river strand,
Where Hans, who followed in dark dismay,
    Could hear her vow,
    His angry vrouw,
"I'll wash and wash till the Judgment Day!"

Along a river that leaped in flame
The Sailing Witches of Salem came.
(They ride the waters, that evil crew,
Wherever the Duyvil hath work to do.)
And every witch in a washtub sat,
And every witch had a coal-black cat
That steered the course with a supple tail,
    A shift for sail,
    A shell to bale,
A thread to reef when the wind blew strong,
A broom to whurry the bark along.

They hailed the vrouw on her spit of sand;
She waved them back with a soapy hand.
Cried one whose face was a Chinese mask,
"This dame is sworn to a goodly task!

Come, friends that ride on the crested swell,
We'll charm the spot with a lasting spell
    That here she'll stay
    And scour away,
And never rest till the Judgment Day!"
With cries to Satan and Beelzebub
They shaped the cape like an upturned tub!—
Beneath its dome and the shifting sands
That busy vrouw at her washtub stands,
    While day and night
    She bends her might
To scrub the fur of a black cat white!

When down the river the norther scuds
The waves are flecked with the rising suds.
When clouds roll black as a Dutchman's hat
You'll hear the wail of the injured cat!
    So heed her fall,
    Good housewives all,
And take this truth from a ragged song—
That super-cleanliness *may* go wrong!

THE HOUSE OF BLAZES

(A Modern Legend of Spuyten Duyvil)

Where Spuyten Duyvil's waves environ
  Manhattan's stern and rock-bound shore
With fume and flame of molten iron
  A foundry's chimneys blaze and roar.

Upon a northward promontory
  The "House of Blazes" stands in pride—
A tavern famed in local story,
  Where grimy furnace-men abide.

Now, one of these, in proud elation,
  Despatched a letter o'er the foam.
And bitter grief and consternation
  That missive caused in Patrick's home!

"Och! Mother av the Saints in glory!"
  The wail arose as Nora read:
"Sure, Pathrick's gone to purgathory!
  He niver wrote that he was dead!

"'Me job is ahl I c'uld desire,'
  Sez he, 'though somewhat warrm I feel
Wid heapin' coal to feed the fire
  An' makin' pies av red-hot steel.

"'The boss is jist the kind that plazes,
  And ahl me mates is mighty civil.
I'm dwellin' in the House av Blazes,
  And right forninst the Spittin' Divil!'"

ZENGER THE PRINTER

IN 1735, under the Administration of Gov. William Cosby, John Peter Zenger, publisher of *The New York Weekly Journal*, was prosecuted for libel mainly because of a bitter satirical review of Cosby's corrupt government that had appeared in his paper. The proceedings were conducted with the greatest unfairness. Zenger's attorneys were expelled from the bar. But on the day of the trial Andrew Hamilton, an old and eminent lawyer from Philadelphia, undertook the defense. "Shall not the oppressed have even the right to complain?" he demanded. "Shall the press be silenced that evil governors may have their way?"

Although the chief justice charged the jury to convict on the ground that an attack on a governing official was libelous whether the statements made therein were true or false, the jury boldly disregarded the charge and declared the defendant "Not guilty" amid the cheers of the audience.

This was the first successful assertion of the liberty of the press at a time when in the cities of Europe and America thought and speech were severely restricted.

ZENGER THE PRINTER

ZENGER the Printer, through storm and stress,
  Deaf to a sycophant Council's rage,
Doggedly toiled at his wooden press
  Building his monument, page by page,

Telling of tyranny's foul disgrace,
  Rousing the spirit that never dies,
Shouting for right in the market-place,
  Speaking the truth in a world of lies!

Vexing the governor's pampered fold,
  Scourging with irony's stinging whip,
Showing how justice was bought and sold;
  Phrasing the wrath of the curling lip.

Wrongfully haled through the public street,
  Wrathfully flung on the dungeon floor,
Grimly he published that galling sheet
  Out "through the hole in the prison door."

Vain were the wiles of a servile judge
  Twisting to evil the wholesome laws!
Vain was the governor's heavy grudge!
  Gallant old Hamilton pled his cause:

"Men of Manhattan! your fateful word
  Curses or blesses the coming time!
Say!—shall the downtrodden die unheard?
  What of your freedom if Truth be crime!"

Nobly the men of a free-born strain
  Answered the note of that noble plea,
Cleaving the truth-teller's futile chain—
  Freeing the weapon that made them free!

        .   .   .   .   .

Zenger the Printer—his work is done;
  Soft be his slumber. Through storm and stress
Guard we the prize of the fight he won—
  Bulwark of Freedom, a fearless press!

.

THE RIVER

What may the gray gull know
  Ere the rolling sun is high
Of the wakened world below
  His road in the winnowed sky?

The song of the crowded streets,
  The throng of the wharf and quay,
The tryst of ships where the river meets
  The burst of the gladdened sea.

Where the smoke-wreaths lift and melt,
  Where the mainsail flaps and fills,
And Hudson heaves like a wampum belt
  On the breast of the strong, red hills.

What may the nighthawk view
  As the great wings cleave their way
Through the gemmed arc's deeper blue
  To the haunt of his midnight prey?

The fairy lamps that show
  On masthead, shrouds, and spars;
The million lights of the town that glow
  Like a bank of welded stars;

And the flare of red abaft,
  And the flash of the green abeam,
And the glow-worm glare of the dragon craft
  That glide on the sable stream.

BUTTERMILK CHANNEL

"BUTTERMILK CHANNEL" is the name
still attached to the strait between Red
Hook on the Brooklyn shore and Governor's
Island. Some hold that the passage was so called
because of the buttermilk which, with other prod-
uce, the country wives were wont to bring across
it in fleets of market-boats on their way to New
York. Other legends, however, indicate that the
name was sometimes sportively applied to the

broader passage of the East River, and there is a
tale to the effect that it commemorates the re-
sourcefulness of the adventurous daughter of a
Long Island farmer when overtaken by a sudden
storm that raised a great commotion in the narrow channel.
13

BUTTERMILK CHANNEL

"Pray tarry, Nancy Blossom,
  With your freight of corn-in-silk
And your chickens and your cheeses
  And your cans of buttermilk!
Wait the morning with your gossip
  In her cabin on the strand;
Bid that lazy darky Mingo
  Draw the market-boat to land;
For the river channel's brawling,
  And the windy heavens frown,
And you'll never reach Manhattan
  'Fore the sun goes down!"

But Nancy had her errand
  And the market wouldn't wait,
So she oared the heavy wherry
  Through the currents of the strait.
Then the tempest broke above her!
  And the chickens squawked in fright;
And the little darky Mingo
  Fairly turned from black to white

[180]

As he chattered, "Laws-a-massy!
  Wuz dis nigger bawn to drown?
Oh, we'll nebber reach Manhattan
  'Fore de sun goes down!"

Then she cuffed that little darky
  Till she taught him to behave;
And they poured a can of buttermilk
  Upon the saucy wave;
And the roughness of the channel
  Grew as smooth as watered silk,
As the angry tide was tempered
  By the mildness of the milk.
So they made the land in safety
  'Mid the cheers of half the town
In the harbor of Manhattan
  'Fore the sun went down.

When the bleak nor'easter blusters,
  When the summer tempests roar
And their host of prankish goblins
  Bend the masts along the shore,
When the wind-lashed wave is scurried
  Down the river to the Bay,
How the surges of the channel
  Froth and foam with milk and whey,

All to honor Nancy Blossom
  Who achieved this high renown
When she crossed to old Manhattan
  'Fore the sun went down!

A CITY GARDEN

Sun-warmed, where Hudson meets the sea,
    My motley-blossomed croft is sown—
A desert inn that cheers the bee
    Astray amid our wastes of stone—

Where pansies raise their velvet heads,
    Where lilies nod to hollyhocks
Across the sweet-alyssum beds;
    And tiger-bells and four-o'clocks,

Right neighborly, together grow—
    The wild and tame, the red and white;
And here I spend the hour of glow
    Ere moths and bats bring in the night.

And here my chair's a ducal throne;
    I rule a fief in Fairyland,
Though scarce to any serf is known
    My puissant, scepter-wielding hand.

Unchecked, his subterrene abode
   That Earth-gnome Worm may dig with zeal,
Nor shall I balk the Ogre Toad
   Who marks him for a horrid meal!

Those gay Zingaras of the breeze,
   The air-delighting Butterflies,
Have come to woo my trellised peas
   That mock so well their forms and dyes.

I know yon dart of emerald light
   That shakes the arbor's dewy shower!
The Humming-bird, bold errant knight,
   Is tilting with the trumpet-flower!

Unthanked, unknown, aloof, benign,
   By wayward whim alone controlled,
Like him that ruled in ease divine
   The careless, lawless Age of Gold,

So do I hold Saturnian reign
   Till one transcending day, I ween,
Shall welcome to her leal domain
   My Suzeraine—the Faery Queen.

BOWLING GREEN

THE little half-acre park on lower Broadway just north of the Custom-House has preserved its identity through many vicissitudes. First an Indian camping-site and council-place, then part of a parade-ground, next a bowling-green, and finally, though under widely varied auspices, a park for the privileged few or the general public, it has been intimately connected with many of the most significant events of the city's history.

Known in the earliest days as the "plain before the fort" and even then largely devoted to recreation, it was in the year of Washington's birth leased for the consideration of "one peppercorn per annum" to three gentlemen "in order to make a Bowling Green there." It was thus the first officially authorized park in the city. In 1772 it is described in the diary of John Adams as "A beautiful ellipsis of land, railed in with solid iron, in the center of which is a statue of his majesty on horseback, very large, of solid lead gilded with gold, standing on a pedestal of marble, very high." It was this leaden statue that a few years later was pulled down by his Majesty's rebellious subjects and run into bullets dedicated to the discomfiture of his Majesty's troops. The railing that still surrounds the green is said to be the original fence mentioned by Adams; but tradition has it that the iron uprights were formerly surmounted with decorative crowns which were broken off by the mob that dethroned the leaden statue of his Majesty King George III.

BOWLING GREEN

A PLEASANT breadth of open space
In wastes of stone, a breathing-place
For dusty toil, though ages roll
Unchanged it spreads a verdant scroll
Whereon is writ, for knowing eyes,
The legend of a city's rise.
Rule prince or people, king or queen,
Still Bowling Green is Bowling Green.

For here, before the Dutchman came,
The Red Man lit his council-flame
To plan the hunt or ambuscade;
And here his dark-eyed children played.
Where now De Peyster's image stands
The simple sachems gave their lands
For trinkets—easy victims fit
For such as crafty Minuit.

Next rose Kryn Frederyck's bastioned fort.
Before the northward sally-port
The soldiers drilled—a gallant breed
Of men that held the Yankee, Swede,

[187]

And Weckquaesgeek in high disdain.
Upon this level, then "The Plaine,"
Van Twiller broached the foaming keg,
Stout Peter stumped on timber leg.

Here drovers sold the flock's increase;
The sullen savage sued for peace;
The young folk came, with dances gay
And garlands, bringing in the May,
While elders nodded, sage and bland,
And lovers rambled hand in hand—
Till English guns in churlish rage
Knelled out our city's Golden Age.

Then, richly turfed and weeded clean,
The gentry laid the level green,
Alluring sport-delighting souls
To cast the jack and hurl the bowls.
And here, as loyal hearts decreed,
King George bestrode a leaden steed,
Till hot rebellion spurned the Crown
And horse and king went crashing down.

Thrice welcome, Peace! The British drum
Hath beat retreat; and see! they come!

With heads erect and muskets true
The tattered troops in buff and blue—
The men that crossed the Delaware
And trapped the Hessian in his lair—
The men of York, of Monmouth plain,
Who marched with Greene, who charged with
    Wayne,

Who fought the war of seven years,
Who whipped the Redcoat Grenadiers—
With swinging stride come marching in,
And all the air is wild with din;
While, strong of limb and stout of soul,
Van Arsdale climbs the well-greased pole
And wrenches down the crimson rag
And sets on high the starry flag!

This bit of turf that woos the sun
The stately step of Washington
Hath pressed; and Fulton knew it well;
And Irving loved its hallowed spell.
It knows the visions, strifes, and tears
And joys of thrice a hundred years.
Unchanged amid a changing scene,
The city's heart is Bowling Green.

Revolu-
tionary
Period

MARY MURRAY OF MURRAY HILL

"BELMONT" was the name given by Lindley Murray to his mansion that stood on the height called by the Dutch "the Incleberg," but now known as "Murray Hill," in the neighborhood of what is now Park Avenue and Thirty-seventh Street.

The Murray estate lay in the direct line of march of the British forces under Sir William Howe, when, on September 15, 1776, having effected a landing at Kip's Bay on the East River about Thirty-fourth Street, they advanced across the island and northward in the wake of the re-treating Americans. A picturesque tradition tells that the strategic hospitality of Mary Murray, delaying the British general, enabled Putnam and Aaron Burr to withdraw Silliman's brigade and Knox's artillery from a perilous position in the city to the southward.

MARY MURRAY OF MURRAY HILL

THE Lady of Belmont looked out to the east:
  The smoke of the battle was wafted aside;
The shattering roar of the cannon had ceased;
  The British flotilla swept over the tide.

And on came the gallant battalions in red
  With glimmer of steel and victorious cheers;
The hills of Manhattan re-echoed their tread—
  The conquering march of the King's Grenadiers.

The Lady of Belmont looked south to the sea;
  Manhattan's green valleys were spread to her
      ken;
"And whose may that column of riflemen be
  Now plain on the hillside, now hid in the glen?"

"'Tis Putnam's! Gray Putnam, to dangers anew
  He carries the scars of the Indian fights!
But where may the doughty old hero win through
  To Washington's army encamped on the
      Heights?

Mary Murray of Murray Hill

"For, barring his path, moves the army of Howe—
  Then Howe must be halted whatever the cost!
No valor can save the old general now;
  'Tis Howe must be halted, or Putnam is lost!"

The Lady of Belmont came down from her tower
  As Howe at her gateway his battle-steed reined.
"Now rest thee, Sir William," she cried, "for an
      hour!
  Thy warfare is over, the laurel is gained.

"And since thou hast conquered my friends with
      the sword,
  The meed of a victor must fall to thy share;
Then sit, if thou wilt, at a true rebel's board
  And taste, if thou wilt, of our good rebel fare."

Then light laughed Sir William and leaped to the
      ground
  (And still, at his word, stood the glittering ranks);
He bowed to the lady in homage profound,
  In phrases right courtly he spake her true thanks.

And long had he tarried her bounty to taste,
  For rich was her larder and merry was she,
When up rode an orderly spurring in haste:
  "Ill tidings, ill tidings, Sir William!" cried he.

[197]

"For Putnam hath slipped through the gap in our
    line!
  He snapped at our vanguard, the crafty old fox,
And, flaunting his flag with its evergreen pine,
  Is off to the rebels encamped on the rocks!"

Oh, wroth was Sir William, but sweetly he smiled,
  And murmured, full knightly, "Fair Lady, I
    fear
The fox stole away as the hounds were beguiled.
  Kind hostess, thy bounty hath cost us too dear!"

UNCLE SAM TO JOHN BULL

John Bullikins, my jo, John,
  We've known each other long.
I've sometimes thought you right, John,
  And often thought you wrong.
We've had our little tiffs, John;
  Yet, whether friend or foe,
I've nursed a high regard for you,
  John Bullikins, my jo.

John Bullikins, my jo, John,
  When all is said and done,
A better friend than you, John,
  Is not beneath the sun.
You've planted noble realms, John,
  Where men may freely grow;
I wouldn't lose you for the world,
  John Bullikins, my jo.

John Bullikins, my jo, John,
  What bunglers we have been!—
For I'm a bungler, too, John,
  Which makes us closer kin.

[199]

We'll somehow blunder through, John;
  Then humbly we will go
To school together, hand in hand,
  John Bullikins, my jo.

HAARLEM HEIGHTS

HISTORIANS of the Revolution have generally underestimated the importance of the Battle of Haarlem Heights, the lively encounter between detachments of the King's troops and Washington's forces, September 16, 1776, upon the hills extending south from West One Hundred and Thirtieth Street, now sometimes called the "Acropolis of New York."

While this skirmish was in the main an affair of outposts, it was the first fight in which the

Americans defeated their opponents in the open field, and the victory, though barren of direct results, was an inspiration to the disheartened soldiers and was hailed bv them as an earnest of ultimate success.

HAARLEM HEIGHTS

Captain Stephen Brown of Knowlton's Connecticut
Rangers tells of the affair of September 16, 1776.

THEY'VE turned! they've fought! Good-by, King
    George,
  Despite your hireling band!
Our 'prentice lads have borne a brunt;
  Our farmer boys will stand!

Though Peace may lag and Fortune flag,
  The fight's as good as won;
We've made them yield in open field!
  We've seen the Redcoats run!

Our Rangers sallied forth at dawn
  With Knowlton at their head
To rout the British pickets out
  And 'change a pound o' lead.

We gave them eight brisk rounds apiece
  And, fighting, hurried back
For, eighteenscore, the Light-armed Corps
  Were hot upon our track.

Along the vale of Bloomingdale
  They pressed our scant array;
They swarmed the crag and jeered our flag
  Across the Hollow Way.

Their flankers hooted, "Hark, away!"
  Their buglers, from the wall,
In boastful vaunt and bitter taunt
  Brayed forth the hunting-call.

Oh, sound of shame! It woke a flame
  In every sunburnt face;
And every soul was hot as coal
  To cleanse the foul disgrace;

Ay, some that blenched on Brooklyn Heights
  And fled at Turtle Bay
Fair wept for wrath, and thronged my path
  And clamored for the fray.

Our general came spurring!
  (There rolled a signal drum);
His eye was bright, he reared his height,
  He knew the time had come.

He gave the word to Knowlton
  That led our own command,
The pick of green Connecticut—
  And Leitch with Weedon's band

Of tall Virginia riflemen,
  Free hunters of the deer,
To round the braggart Briton's flank
  And take him in the rear.

We left the dell, we scaled the fell,
  And up the crest we sprang,
When, crackling sharp along the scarp,
  A deadly volley rang,

And down went Leitch of Weedon's band
  Deep hurt, but dauntless still;
And down went Knowlton, sword in hand—
  The sword of Bunker Hill.

I raised his head. But this he said,
  Death-wounded as he lay.
"Lead on the fight! My hurt is light
  If Freedom win the day!"

In open rank we struck their flank,
  And oh! the fight was hot!
Up came the Hessian Yägers,
  Up came the kilted Scot,

Up came the men of Linsingen,
  Von Donop's Grenadiers!
But swift we sped the whistling lead
  About the Dutchmen's ears.

They buckled front to Varnum's brunt,
  We crumpled up their right,
And, driving back the crimson wrack,
  We swept along the height.

The helmet of the Hessian
  Is tumbled in the wheat!
The tartan of the Highlander
  Shall be his winding-sheet!

In mingled rout we drove them out
  From orchard, field, and glen;
In goodly case it seemed to chase
  Our "hunters" home again!

We flaunted in their faces
  The flag they thought to scorn,
And left them with a wild "Hurrah!"
  To choke their hunting-horn!

Upon a ledge embattled
  Above the river strand
We dug the grave for Knowlton
  And Leitch of Weedon's band;

And though our star through stress of war
  Desert this island throne,
Upon that ledge remains the pledge
  That we will claim our own!

THE BLOCK-HOUSE IN THE PARK

The North Wind storms my rugged front,
  The ivy scales my southern wall;
I never knew the crashing brunt
  Of musketry or cannon-ball.

When armies met in battle-shock,
  When smoke of navies rolled afar,
Men made me strong on living rock;
  I frowned with guns awaiting war;

Awaiting war that never came,
  A virgin fortress still I stand;
But now, unscathed by hostile flame,
  I guard a gate of Fairyland.

For, while my gloomy watch I stood,
  Unmarked the leafy marvel grew;
Behind me spread the mystic wood—
  A place of dreams where dreams are true;

Where low winds move the tasseled fir,
  Where lilacs breathe, where brown bees hum,
Where old men tell of days that were,
  Where lovers talk of days to come;

Where boyish cohorts, undismayed,
  Deploy beneath the friendly trees
To take my cliffs by escalade.
  May all their wars be such as these!

THE STORMING OF STONY POINT

LIKE many another good soldier, before and since, Gen. Anthony Wayne strongly objected to a nickname imputing to him the characteristic of rash, headlong courage. As a matter of fact, his popular title, "Mad Anthony," is said to have been fastened upon him by a grumbling Irish soldier whom he had severely disciplined. It is certain that Wayne was a strategist as well as a dashing fighter. His most brilliant exploit, the storming of Stony Point, was carefully planned and perfectly executed; and Wayne's calm courage is shown by the fact that he led the storming party in person in spite of a strong, though happily false, premonition that he would be killed in the attack.

THE STORMING OF STONY POINT

HIGHLANDS of Hudson! ye saw them pass,
  Night on the stars of their battle-flag,
Threading the maze of the dark morass
  Under the frown of the Thunder Crag;

Flower and pride of the Light-armed Corps,
  Trim in their trappings of Buff and Blue,
Silent, they skirted the rugged shore,
  Grim in the promise of work to do.

"Cross ye the ford to the moated rock!
  Let not a whisper your march betray!
Out with the flint from the musket-lock!
  Now!—let the bayonet find the way!"

"Halt!" rang the sentinel's challenge clear.
  Swift came the shot of the waking foe.
Bright flashed the ax of the pioneer
  Smashing the abatis, blow on blow.

15   [211]

Little they tarried for British might!
  Little they recked of the Tory jeers!
Laughing, they swarmed to the crested height,
  Steel to the steel of the Grenadiers!

Storm King and Dunderberg! wake once more,
  Sentinel giants of Freedom's throne,
Massive and proud! to the eastern shore
  Bellow the watchword: "The fort's our own!"

Echo the cannon's triumphant peal!
  Shout for the hero who led his band,
Swept on a billow of burnished steel
  Over the parapet, "spear in hand!"

Laughing, they swarmed to the crested height,
Steel to the steel of the Grenadiers!

OLD TRINITY

This was a merchant, and that was a belle,
There lies a statesman—you know how he fell.

Under that monument fronting the street
Rests the young sailor, who, spurning defeat,

In a lost battle, and with his last prayer
Gave us a watchword to challenge Despair.

Tory and Patriot camp side by side;
Truce of the turf to their rancor and pride!

Look toward the river. The stone at your feet
Shelters a blade of his Majesty's fleet,

Gallant and gay, when the red-coated leaven
Troubled our city, in 'seventy-seven.

What of his ending?—(the daisies may know
More that is silence)—a word and a blow!

[215]

Then, a locked room in the tavern, the gloom
Flickered with candles; the whisper of doom;

Bicker and ring of encountering steel,
Panting of bosoms, the stamp of the heel,

Feint, circle, parry, lunge, counter, and carte!—
Dead! like a man, with a thrust through the heart!

What was the cause?   Ah, you question in vain!
Dorothy, Annabel, Phyllis, or Jane,

Queen of assemblies and toast of the bold,
Somewhere she slumbers in Trinity's mold.

Search in your heart if you seek to descry
That which is hidden!—the passions that lie

Buried in Earth with her grasses above—
Sorrow and Ecstasy, Hatred and Love.

THE FATE OF THE HESSIAN

WHERE the City Prison now frowns upon Center Street a beautiful pond once allured the angler and swimmer in summer and the skater in winter. This little lake was called by the Dutch "Kalch Hoeck," because of the vast quantity of shells that lined its shores, and later, by the English, the Fresh Water or Collect Pond. Originally it was a place of pure delight; but, perhaps because of sinister incidents such as the hanging of some of the alleged participants in the Negro Plot on the island in its center, ill-omened rumors spread to darken the fair fame of the little inland sea. It was whispered that the pond was bottomless and that uncanny monsters lurked in its dark depths, ready to seize the unwary bather—a story that was countenanced by several fatalities.

Early in the last century a smoke-breathing monster did indeed swim upon the surface of the lake, for it was here that Robert Fulton launched the model of his first steamboat. Abuse and neglect finally changed the once bright sheet of water into a foul and evil-odored pool, and about 1810 the Collect Pond was drained and filled in and disappeared from the city map, to be recalled only in a few traditions such as that which follows.

THE FATE OF THE HESSIAN

A LEGEND OF THE COLLECT POND

WHO blusters along with his clattering blade,
    In green regimentals and brass-fronted helm,
With blackened mustaches, and hair in pomade
    And powder—as proud as a Prussian?—the
        schelm!

Who ruffles with bullies and frightens the fops?
    Who growls at the tavern, gruff-voiced as a bear:
"*Sturmwetter un Hagel! Schnell! Hier mit mein'*
    schnapps?"
    Why, Friedrich von Heusen, the Hessian chas-
        seur;

The scorn of the Briton who gives him his pay;
    The tyrant and dread of the Tory recruits,
The bugbear of children, who shrink from the way
    And quake at the creak of his heavy-soled boots,

For foul are the rumors that darken the door
   Of Sugar-House Prison—that Keep of Despair,
Where poor, captive rebels are dead by the score
   In Friedrich the Jailer's benevolent care!

The Hessian caroused at the inn till the gray
   Stole over the rose where the sun had gone down,
Then strolled through the fields to the Collect
      that lay
   Embosomed in meads, to the north of the town—

A lake that was loved by the angler, who claimed
   The crimson-flecked trout of its crystalline waves,
But shunned after twilight, for monsters unnamed
   Arose from the depths of its bottomless caves.

As Friedrich glanced out toward its centering isle
   He spied in the thicket, half hidden from view,
A form, worn and wasted and lean as a file,
   In rags of rebellion—the Buff and the Blue.

"Ho, kerl!" jeered the jailer, "thy garments are torn!
   Thou runaway rebel, come hither, I say!
Thy comrades are lonely, thy prison's forlorn.
   No? *Dummkopf!* I'll fetch thee; and then shalt
      thou pay!"

He cast down his helmet in ireful haste,
  He kicked off his jack-boots, he tore off his coat,
And, girding the big-hilted sword to his waist,
  He splashed in the lake with a curse in his throat.

The waters, as black as the glass of Lorraine,
  Were stirred from their depths with a heave and
      a roll;
Fright-stricken, the Hessian surged forward—in
      vain!
  The Fiend of the Collect had come for his toll!

He struggled, but silent, resistless as Fate
  A huge scaly arm strained his thews, fold on
      fold,
He screamed in his madness; remorseless as Hate
  A great, evil claw gripped his throat in its hold.

The bubbles rose, sobbing, then ceased and were
      still;
  The ripple was hushed on the shell-littered shore;
The darkness descended on river and hill;
  And field, camp, and prison knew Friedrich no
      more!

THE INN: AN OLD EPITAPH

Post-haste we ride the road of men
From shadow through to shade again,
But rein, to breathe or tighten girth,
At that old inn yclept "The Earth."
There some delay to dine and sup,
While some but taste a stirrup-cup;
And some have ease and ample fare,
And some find little comfort there.
His score is large who bides a day;
Who soonest goes hath least to pay.

THE DYCKMAN HOUSE

NORTH of the line of Dyckman Street to
Spuyten Duyvil Kill stretched the domain
ruled by the dynasties of Jan Dyckman and Jan
Nagel, and ruled in neighborly amity save for the
comparatively brief duration of a feud arising
from a violation of manorial ethics—the Nagel
goose strayed into the Dyckman corn and was bit-
ten by the Dyckman dog. For a time the feeling
aroused by this episode was so bitter that the trans-
action of public business was hampered by the re-
fusal of the heads of the two houses to sit on the
same administrative board. But the breach was
soon healed. In fact, a year after the death of
Nagel, in 1689, Jan Dyckman married the widow
of his late feudal brother, and the second generation of both clans was reared under the same roof.
Yet the Dyckmans appear to have been the stronger
breed, and "Dyckman" still remains a name to
conjure by in northern Manhattan. The original
Dyckman homestead was burned during the Revo-

lution; but the farm-house built by William Dyck-man and his sons in 1783 on their return from the war and exile still stands on the west side of Broad-way at Two Hundred and Fourth Street, restored and converted into a public memorial of the past through the generosity of the inheritors of the Dyckman blood and spirit.

THE DYCKMAN HOUSE

PLAIN as the brass of an old sword-hilt
Is the tale of the house that the Dyckmans built.

In Charles the Second's jovial reign,
Jan, the first of the Dyckman strain,
Fair-haired, ruddy, strong, and shrewd,
Cleared the soil, and his hardy brood
Killed the wolves in their rocky lairs,
Turned the loam with iron shares.

Full a hundred years had fled;
Well the Dyckman race had sped;
Sweet their orchards, broad their farms
When Freedom called true men to arms.
They nursed no doubts of the need of force;
They did their part as a thing of course.
Forth they sallied, boy and man.
William, head of the Dyckman clan,
Took the field, and his three good sons
Marched along with their flintlock guns—

Abraham bold and Michael keen
And blithe young William, aged thirteen.

Through the war with its changing tides
The Dyckmans fought in the gallant Guides.
Their chronicles may still be found
In the blood-stained roll of the Neutral Ground,
And yellowed, time-worn records tell
How sturdy Abraham Dyckman fell,
Raiding the camp of De Lancey's corps,
And how young William paid that score.

Peace at last!—In full retreat
Sounded the tramp of alien feet
Quitting the isle we love;—and then
The Dyckmans came to their own again.
But the camping foe had left their land
Bare as the back of a baby's hand.
Waste were the fields and the orchards, too;
Burned was the home in which they grew.

The Dyckman breed were men of force;
They took their task as a thing of course.
Again they plowed their wasted leas,
Again they set their orchard trees;

With toughened timbers, marked by fire,
From tumbled barn and ruined byre,
They raised the framework, strongly planned,
Of this old house. Long may it stand
A monument for coming years
Of the last of the flower of the pioneers.

For in this brave old house survives
The lesson blazed by its builders' lives:

"Be true; and keep, whate'er befall,
The faith that each man owes to all.
Be strong; for strength shall purge you clear
Of all mean hatreds born of Fear.
Then, should the years that hither press
Bring other days of storm and stress,
A race of clean-limbed, clear-eyed men
Shall look the world in the face again."
16

OUR COLONEL

Deep loving, well knowing
  His world and its blindness,
A heart overflowing
  With measureless kindness,

Undaunted in labor
  (And Death was a trifle),
Steel-true as a saber,
  Direct as a rifle,

All Man in his doing,
  All Boy in his laughter,
He fronted, unruing,
  The Now and Hereafter,

A storm-battling cedar,
  A comrade, a brother—
Oh, such was our leader,
  Beloved as no other!

When weaker souls faltered
  His courage remade us,
Whose tongue never paltered,
  Who never betrayed us.

His hand on your shoulder
  All honors exceeding,
What breast but was bolder
  Because he was leading!

And still in our trouble,
  In peace or in war-time,
His word shall redouble
  Our strength as aforetime.

When wrongs cry for righting
  No odds shall appal us;
To clean, honest fighting
  Again he will call us,

And, cowboys or doughboys,
  We'll follow his drum, boys,
Who never said, "Go, boys!"
  But always said, "Come, boys!"

[229]

A RAID OF THE NEUTRAL GROUND

DURING the greater part of the Revolutionary War the British lines were at King's Bridge, at the upper end of Manhattan Island, the American outposts about thirty miles to the north. The No Man's Land in between, the lovely hill-and-valley region of Westchester, was known as "the Neutral Ground," presumably because there was more mixed fighting to the square mile in that locality than anywhere else in the thirteen states. The rallying-place of the American partizans was a stone building known as Young's house, not far from White Plains, which commanded the road 'eading down the Valley of the Nepperhan. Young's house was burned by the enemy; and the following ballad tells the tale of a retaliatory attack by the Westchester Guides and other Revolutionary forces, upon De Lancey's Royal Refuge Corps encamped under the guns of Fort Number Eight on the heights overlooking the Harlem River.

As the old campaigner who tells the story of the

raid is, like all of the Revolutionary party, so bitter against the Tories, it is well to remember that these American loyalists were, to a large extent, men of high principle, honestly devoted to their cause, and that the infant Republic lost much of its best blood by their wholesale migration to Canada at the close of the war.

A RAID OF THE NEUTRAL GROUND

"Up! bully boys of the Nepperhan!
  Gather! ye troopers, grim and rough;
Ye of the hardy homespun clan,
  Ye who have trained in the Blue and Buff.
Come from the Highlands, grandly free,
  Barring the stream to the baffled foe;
Come from your farms by the Tappan Zee,
  Come from the Vale of Pocantico!"
Dark of the moon; and shadows deep
  Curtain the road on field and ridge;
Laggardly watch the redcoats keep,
  Calling the word at Dyckman's Bridge.

Down in a dell by the Sawmill ford
  Fourscore men to the muster throng;
Scarred are some by the British sword,
  Scarred are some by the deeper wrong:
Murdoch—he of the Monmouth fray;
  Dircksen, wreck of a massive bulk,
One of the hundreds racked away,
  Starved in the *Jersey's* prison hulk;

"Up! bully boys of the Nepperhan!
Gather! ye troopers, grim and rough."

Dyckman, breathing his dead boy's name;
  Young, God knoweth, a vengeful man,
Brooding and dark since the Tory flame
  Blackened his home by the Nepperhan.
Oh, give and take is the way of war,
  And of cloven helmets our own swords tell;
But the turncoat curs of the Tory corps
  We hate as we hate the gates of hell.

Only the beaver, sunk from view,
  Watched us pass with a furtive eye;
Only the owl of Mosholu
  Challenged us as we skirted by;
Only the stars, through a drift of gray
  Silently beckoning, led us straight
There where De Lancey's Tories lay
  Under the guns of Number Eight.

"Brands!" And the bridge upon Haarlem's breast
  Melts in a broken chain of fire;
Every hut has a flaming crest,
  Every shack is a blazing pyre.
Blundering out to the lurid night
  Rally the shreds of the hated corps;
Speak to them! gun of the Trenton fight,
  Bell-muzzled piece of the Indian War!

[235]

Reavers and harriers, each and all,
  Traitors with blood of their country wet—
Ply them with rifle and musket-ball!
  At them with saber and bayonet!

Loosen the horses! Burn the hay!
  Kill whom ye must and take whom ye can,
For the Yägers are up on the King's Bridge Way.
  So it's back! through the Valley of Nepperhan!
Three miles up through the well-known glade,
  Helmeted Yägers hard on our track,
Laughing, we turned at our ambuscade,
  Hurling the Hessians staggering back.

Dark were our deeds of the steel and brand?
   Aye. But they wearied a stubborn foe,
Held him at bay, while our leader planned,
   Cautious and wise, for the final blow.
Judge us fairly, if judge ye may;
   Freed is our country of hostile ban;
Redcoat and Hessian have had their day;
   Peace rules the Vale of the Nepperhan.

WASHINGTON IN WALL STREET

Sublime, where traffic's billows beat
A nation's wealth about his feet,
He stands; upon the surging street
   He looks benignly down.
He hears the distant, wall-hid sea,
The silver chime of Trinity,
And, voicing passion, grief, or glee,
   Our million-throated town.

And, up and down, our tasks we ply
With rapid step and heedless eye,
Alert alone to sell and buy;
   But when the day grows dim,
When evening brings its sweet release
From toil and care, when tumults cease,
When twilight crowns his brow with peace,
   The children come to him.

Rejoicing, free, in careless grace
They climb the massy granite base;

Unawed, they view that noble face,
   They swarm the brazen knees
Whose polished surface now denies
The gray of age that artists prize;
But more than art is all that lies
   In love of such as these.

What matters race, or hue, or creed?
Though born to wealth or born to need,
Or sprung of poor plebeian seed
   Or proud patrician stem,
From lowly hut or lordly hall—
By these his land shall rise or fall.
His hand outstretched above them all,
   Their father blesses them.

FORT TRYON

FORT TRYON, at One Hundred and Ninety-sixth Street and Fort Washington Avenue, overlooking the Hudson, was the key to the northern defenses of Fort Washington; and its capture by the Hessians under Rahl and Knyphausen, after a desperate defense, November 16, 1776, gave Manhattan Island to the enemy for the remainder of the war.

FORT TRYON

AGAIN there's a golden haze
  On the shadow of Hudson glades;
Again are the leaves ablaze
  On the breast of the Palisades;
Again from the loft of the wind-swept stair
  We watch how the sea-gulls fly,
And we drink full draughts of the sparkling air
  From the deep blue cup of sky.

Look south where the ocean rills,
  Look east to the dancing Sound,
Look north to the swelling hills
  And the vales of the Neutral Ground!
From the Mart of the Sea where the millions toil
  To the heights in the farthest ken
There is never a rood of the sacred soil
  But was bought with the blood of men.

The red that the woodland shows,
  The swell of the city's hum,
Seem the garb of advancing foes
  And the roll of a phantom drum;

The glimmer that leaps to the parapet
   As we look toward the Northern Town
Is the shimmer of helmet and bayonet
   As the Hessian troops come down.

Once more swing the hostile boats
   In the eddies of Haarlem Kill,
While the Cross of the Briton floats
   On the ramparts of Laurel Hill;
And the grass-mantled battlements wake again
   To the whir of the musket-ball
And the shouts of the Maryland Riflemen
   As they close with the hosts of Rahl!

What need that defeat be cloaked?
   They lost; but was theirs the blame
Who fought till their rifles choked
   With the reek of the darted flame?
And the meed of their deaths, of their woes and
      scars
   Is a boon such alone could buy;
See! the stainless Flag of the Clustered Stars
   Rides alone in a peaceful sky!

DECATUR'S TOAST

"Our Country! In her intercourse with foreign nations may she always be right; but, Our Country—Right or Wrong!"—COMMODORE STEPHEN DECATUR, *Norfolk, Virginia, April, 1816.*

Up rose, triumphant, from his seat
    The Bayard of the Sea—
The lion of our laureled fleet,
    The scourge of Barbary;
His glass abrim with bubbling light,
    He pledged that brilliant throng—
"Our Country!—be she ever right;
    Our Country!—right or wrong!"

Then round about the oaken board
    The goblets leaped and rang,
And fervent fingers pressed the sword
    As up the heroes sprang;
No mawkish qualms or doubts had they
    That echoed deep and strong,
"Our Country!—ever right, we pray;
    Our Country—right or wrong!

17   [243]

Too well the stifling mists they knew
    That dimmed the Stars we bore—
The plots of banded traitors, who,
    Amid the stress of war,
Made weightier their nation's woes,
    Till rose the patriot song:
"When face to face with foreign foes,
    Our Country!—right or wrong!"

Stanch lovers of our free domain,
    We strive for truth and right
With honest force of heart and brain
    As God may give us light.
But doubts must yield and ties must break
    When darkening perils throng;
And when the sullen guns awake,
    "Our Country!—right or wrong!"

THE BALLAD OF JOHN PAUL JONES

NO more picturesque figure ever adorned a quarter-deck than Commodore John Paul Jones, whom some English writers even in recent days have insisted on miscalling a "Scotch pirate."

Jones's daring cruise in British waters in 1777-78 spread a terror along the coasts utterly out of proportion to the insignificance of his force—a terror still evidenced by queer old songs of the day and grotesque caricatures representing the rather dapper commodore as a most ruffianly pirate. His chief exploit was the capture of the *Serapis* off Flamborough Head, September 23, 1779, after the most desperate fight between single vessels on record.

Although some recent biographers have claimed for Jones more than history warrants, there is no doubt that he was a dauntless fighter, an able strategist, an admirable seaman, something of a diplomat, and withal a man most punctilious in honor.

[245]

THE BALLAD OF JOHN PAUL JONES

"For Capt. Paul Jones ever loved close fighting."—
BENJAMIN FRANKLIN.

HE hath masted the flag of the crimson bars
    To dance in a gladdened sky.
He hath claimed a salute for the Thirteen Stars,
    And the cannon of France reply.

He hath harried the barks of the Narrow Seas,
    He hath trodden the Scottish ling,
He hath flaunted his rebel blazonries
    In the face of the stubborn king.

From the Frith of Forth through the startled North
    The panic rumor runs,
And the coastguards south into Humber Mouth
    Know the blare of the Yankee guns.

He had cruised that coast for a week, I wis,
    And mickle the woe and loss,
When he was aware of the *Serapis*
    That floated St. George's Cross.

And her sailors laughed: "Ho! merchant craft,
  What cargo have ye got?"
"Have back your jape! We carry grape
  And round and double shot!"

Then the thundering broadsides flashed and roared
  And the musketry sped its rain;
But the second round that the *Richard* poured
  Her great guns burst amain.

There was slaughter and wreck to her quarter-
     deck,
  And the foemen knew her plight;
"Have you struck?" they sang. His answer rang:
  "I have not begun to fight!"

He veered around till his counter ground
  On the bows of the British craft;
He grappled her fast to his mizzenmast,
  He grappled her fore and aft.

Their yards were locked as the horns of stags
  That war on the trampled steep.
They strove in night as the dragons fight
  In the darks of the churning deep.

And gun kissed gun with the kiss of hate
   And the ban of the blazing lip;
And the gunners leant till the rammers went
   Through the ports of the hostile ship.

And shot rent through and splinters flew;
   It was fire and flood and wrack,
Red flame ashine on hissing brine
   And red blood curdling black.

But ever the *Richard's* topmen swept
   The decks of the shrinking foe;
They won their way with the musket-play
   While the Briton raged below.

The sailors clung to the dizzy shrouds
　　And spars that bent and swayed;
Through the open keeps to the powder-heaps
　　They hurled the loud grenade.

A roar went up from the *Serapis*,
　　A roar and a cry of bale,
The smoke-cloud rolled from her shattered hold
　　And she leaped like a wounded whale.

A shout went up from the *Richard's* crew
　　As they swarmed o'er the side to strike,
And the moonlight played on the cutlass blade
　　And the flame on the boarding-pike.

A sullen hail from her quarter-deck,
　　A cheer from the Yankee tars;
St. George's Cross must own its loss,
　　To the steel of the Thirteen Stars.

　　　．　　　．　　　．　　　．　　　．

He hath taken his prize to the Texel Roads
　　Where none should work him wrong,
But the British wrath is about his path,
　　And the British arm is strong.

And the Land of the Fen is scant of men;
    Though her people speak him fair,
He must bend his mast ere a week be past,
    For he may not harbor there.

"We know not your stripes and your dancing stars,
    So choose ye, stout John Paul:
Will ye leave your prize where moored she lies,
    Or away 'neath the flag of Gaul?"

"'Tis by evil chance that I leave to France
    What we bought with the blood so red,
But away we'll slip in a weaker ship
    With the free stars tossed o'erhead."

It was black as the maw of a witch's cat
    And the wind was a shrieking gale.
'Twas a murk, murk night, and the waves threshed
            white
    'Neath the strokes of the norther's flail.

"Oh, it's reef your sail to the sweeping gale
    And the threat of the wintry skies,
For we're up and away from the churlish bay
    'Neath the bonniest flag that flies!"

There are twoscore ships of the Channel Fleet
  All alert for the rover dread;
And the king hath told a wealth in gold
  As the price of the "pirate's" head.

But the fleet may rest from a bootless quest
  And the king tell his guineas o'er;
He is running free on the open sea
  And home to the western shore.

          .   .   .   .   .

Though he struck for the right and in open fight
  And he kept his honor clear,
They affront his fame with their lying blame
  And the taunt of "the Buccaneer"!

So we'll drink, "Paul Jones!" and the world may
        hark
  While the clashing beakers peal!
For he took his prize in a sinking bark
  By the sweep of the moonlit steel!

THE OLD "CONSTITUTION"

Before the wind that greets the sun
   She bowled along in glee—
The brave old ship whose cannon won
   The freedom of the sea.

And fifteen stripes and fifteen stars
   She flaunted high in air
When Hull's fierce broadsides raked the spars
   Of England's "Guerrière."

The school where heroes proved their worth
   In gale or battle smoke,
Her masts were pines of mountain birth,
   Her sides were native oak.

And proud in sails without a fleck,
   She rode to meet the foe
When Bainbridge walked her quarter-deck
   A hundred years ago.

FRAUNCES' TAVERN

AT the corner of Broad and Pearl Streets stands
Fraunces' Tavern, now restored, as nearly
as might be, to its condition in the days when
Gen. George Washington made it his head-
quarters. The old mansion was erected early in
the eighteenth century by Stephen or Étienne De
Lancey, and later was purchased by Samuel
Fraunces, who opened it as an inn displaying the
sign of "Queen Charlotte."

Many historic gatherings have been held within
the walls of the old house, but its chief title to
fame is the fact that its Long Room witnessed the
affecting parting of Washington and his generals
at the close of the Revolution.

FRAUNCES' TAVERN

RESTORE, O Thought, whose potent weird
   Recalls the Past on lagging pinion,
The corbeled roof De Lancey reared
   What time Queen Anne maintained dominion.

Away with dust and rattling pave!
   Let all be swarded, green and trim,
And call the river's banished wave
   Again to lap a garden's rim.

How bright with silk and rich brocade,
   With baldric broad and tossing feather.
The Long Room rilled when youth and maid
   Went swinging down the floor together!

Those heavy beams could make avow
   Of all the joys of dance and reel,
Of flirt of fan and courtly bow
   And sudden glint of jealous steel.

But ruthless Traffic claimed the place;
  And swarthy-visaged Landlord Fraunces
Displayed Queen Charlotte's pictured face
  To awe his guests with regal glances.

Then here the traveler reined his beast
  And drank his noggin in the shade,
And merchants met in solemn feast
  To ponder for the weal of trade;

And captains, fresh from siege and plain,
  Rehearsed their tales of savage warring
At Frontenac and Fort Duquesne
  In tones that set the glasses jarring,

And pledged the memory of him
  Who stormed the Heights of Abraham
In bumpers beaded to the brim
  With rousing punch of Rip van Dam.

Oppressed by laws of grievous weight
  And tyrant craft but ill dissembled,
Within these walls, in high debate,
  The "Sons of Liberty" assembled.

In vain they pled for right undone!
    In vain, for hearts were stern and proud—
Till rang the shot of Lexington
    And grimly closed the battle-cloud.

.   .   .   .   .

But hark! the room resounds anew
    With clink of spurs and clank of sabers;
The leader comes to bid adieu
    To those who shared his wars and labors—

To knightly Schuyler, void of stain,
    To rugged Morgan, frank and free,
To faithful Knox and fiery Wayne,
    And dashing Light-Horse Harry Lee.

To all he pledged the cup of grace;
From every eye the tear-drop started;
Each clasped his chief in strong embrace;
In silent grief the heroes parted.

Oh, cherish safe from force unkind,
Though rust consume both sword and pen,
Those ancient walls that hold enshrined
The honest love of gallant men!

Miscel-laneous

THE PALISADES

THE Mahican or Mohegan Indians, a principal tribe of the great Lenni-Lenape or "Original People," had their own version of the origin of their noble river, the Mahican-ittuck, which we call the Hudson, and a version that is partly justified by the observations of geologists. The legend of the river is also connected with another of the creation of the Palisades, those great columns and ramparts of basaltic rock that rise on the western shore of the sacred stream.

THE PALISADES

HEAR an ancient Indian legend told in many a
lodge of yore
Where the great Mahican-ittuck rolls on Mannahatta's shore;

Where across the silent river frown in furrowed
lights and shades
Fire-born basalt, brave with verdure, forest-
crowned, the Palisades.

"Know ye why our corn is golden ere the forest
breaks in flame?
Why our rivers leap with salmon? Why our
woodland stirs with game?

"Children of the Ancient People! over all your
home is blest;
For of all the lands beneath him, yours the
Manitou loved best.

[262]

"High among old hills that knew not council-
flare nor hunter's trail
Slept a lake, unrilled though forests crashed before the northern gale;

"For, upon a central island raised, the mystic
wigwam stood
Where the Mighty Spirit brooded, planning for
his people's good.

"Envious, the Sons of Evil vexed the lake with
frightful dreams
Till the billows, white with terror, stormed the
isle in torrent streams,

"Forced the gateway of the hills, and headlong
to the vale below
Plunged in panic, dashing, tumbling—formed the
river that ye know.

"Rose in wrath the Mighty Spirit; caught and
bound the evil band;
Spake unto the waves and calmed them; led the
river with his hand.

"Where the turbid waters mingled with the brine
of ocean waves,
There the Master flung his captives howling down
the dismal caves.

"Over them his potent magic reared the massive
cliffs that stand
Jailers of the Sons of Evil, wardens of the favored
land.

"Through the bitter Moon of Snowshoes, by your
lodge-flames crouching warm,
Ye may hear the captives wailing to their brothers of the storm;

"But they may not force their prison; nor may
spirit evil-crazed
Ever pass the charmèd ramparts by the hand of
God upraised.

"Hail! ye shaggy-breasted Giants, rugged guards
of field and glade!
Tempest-quelling, stand forever; matchless, change-
less, unafraid!"

UNDER THE PALISADES

Light as a leaf on the lifting swell,
　Balanced by touch of the spruce-wood blades,
Poised like a javelin, floats my shell
　Under the frown of the Palisades.

Molded were they in volcanic fire,
　Up from the bosom of Chaos hurled,
Battlement, pinnacle, column, spire
　Carved by the Chisel that wrought the world.

Clear to their Dunsinane rampart sweep
　Bough-bearing armies of rooted foes;
Bright in their chasms the cascades leap;
　Over their rubble the fox-grape grows.

Long have they guarded the river's flow,
　Summer and winter the ages through,
Watching the argosies come and go—
　Go, like the Indian's frail canoe.

[265]

Proud in the heavens they seem to say,
  Catching my feathering oarblade's gleam,
"What is yon waif of a passing day
  Vexing the rill of our golden stream?"

Cliffs of the eons that woo the sky,
  Furrowed with shadows of world-old thought,
Brood ye in pity on such as I? . . .
  I shall be deathless when ye are naught!

THE DEVIL'S STEPPING-STONES

IT may have been a too intimate acquaintance with the grimmer side of Old World theology that led the early settlers to give over to the powers of evil the fairest lands and waters in their new possessions. "Hell Gate" and "Spuyten Duyvil" mark the eastern and northern limits of Manhattan. Up the Hudson, on the west shore not far beyond Poughkeepsie, is the "Duyvils' Dans-kammer," the Devils' Dancing-chamber. Even placid Long Island Sound figures on old Colonial maps as "the Devil's Belt"; and the irregular, broken reefs that stretch from the base of Great Neck across the Sound to the mainland are to this day known as "the Devil's Stepping-stones."

THE DEVIL'S STEPPING-STONES

A SKY of gold, a sea of blue,
A drowsy day of naught to do;
In pleasant waves our lines we threw
　At anchor as we lay
Where, reaching through the gentle Sound,
Manhasset rears a wooded mound
And Schuyler, grimly cannon-crowned,
　Disputes the narrow way.

Right merrily our angling throve!
By noon we sought a sheltered cove
Where, plunging, joyously we clove
　The waters clear and cold.

Our feast we spread, our songs were sung;
Then, pipes alight, at ease we flung
To harken while our skipper's tongue
    Rehearsed a tale of old.

In rugged lines that vainly strive to reach the
    northern side,
The shell-grown ledges rear their heads above the
    ebbing tide.
There blackfish haunt, and sea-bass love the
    salty flow that drones
Among the clefts—but sailors shun the Devil's
    Stepping-stones.

Long, long before the white man came, Pequot
    traditions tell,
Habbamocko, the Evil One, that spirit wild and
    fell,
Strode forth through fair Connecticut, and, casting
    flame around,
Waged war to gain the fertile vales that skirt
    the northern Sound.

Twelve days the demon strove with men, while
    all the sky was red

With blazing shaft and hurtling brand; and then
    the tyrant fled,
Still battling, east along the strand in hissing
    foam and spray
To yonder jutting spit of land that pierces Pelham
    Bay.

Here, harassed by a hundred foes, the baffled
    fiend forbore;
Across the wave-worn Stepping-stones he reached
    Long Island's shore.

In that far time no boulders rude bespread the
    fertile main,
But through the island shattered crags were thick
    on hill and plain.
At Cold Spring Bay the vengeful fiend heaped
    high a lofty pile
Of all the gathered bones of earth that strewed
    the sandy isle.

Loud laughed the fierce Habbamocko as laughs
    the angry gale!
Across the Sound with mighty arm he hurled the
    craggy hail.

On shore and hill the heavy stones were flung with
  crashing din
To load with sterile bonds the land his prowess
  failed to win.

　　And since that day of flaming shocks
　　　　And fierce, infernal revel,
　　Connecticut has all the rocks—
　　　　Long Island keeps the Devil.

A SEA CHARM

Winds that waft the fisher-fleet
Cool the sands from burning heat!
Trouble not her slender feet,
Wave-worn pebbles!
Crusty crabs both great and small
Where the billows rise and fall,
Quit her path, I charge ye all,
Be not rebels!

Smile above her, azure dome!
Lap her softly, curling foam!
White-ridged combers tumbling home
Rarely laden,

[272]

Rolling in from open sea
Rock her high in giant glee,
Bearing safely back to me
  My mermaiden!

MONTGOMERY'S RETURN

AMONG the general officers in the American army at the beginning of the Revolution none was of greater promise than Richard Montgomery, whose noble bearing, winning manners, and splendid bravery were extolled alike by friend and foe. Montgomery had been but two years married to Janet Livingston at the commencement of hostilities, but he at once offered his services and was placed in command of the ill-fated expedition to Quebec. In a bitter winter campaign with but a small force he captured Montreal and conquered, to quote Edmund Burke, two-thirds of Canada, only to fall, December 31, 1775, leading a desperate assault on Quebec.

In 1818 the general's remains were removed and convoyed down the Hudson to be reinterred in St. Paul's Chapel, New York, near the monument that had been ordered in Paris by Benjamin Franklin. As the funeral barge, floating slowly down the

Hudson to the booming of minute guns, passed Montgomery's home near Rhinebeck, his widow, looking upon the bier, fainted away in the stress of what she afterward said was the proudest and saddest moment of her life.
19

MONTGOMERY'S RETURN

How black the barge of trailing pall
    And nodding sable plume
That Hudson bears by mountain wall
    And fields of golden bloom
A cloud upon the azure flow,
    A shadow in the sun,
To drumhead roll and church-bell toll
    And boom of minute gun!
By night the ruddy beacons flame
    On crested Kaaterskill.
Great heart that beat for Love and Fame
    Why liest thou so still?

How blithe and brave he left his hall
    Beside the Hudson's wave!
He heard his struggling country's call,
    His uttermost he gave.
He bade his bonny bride farewell;
    In wastes of nor'land snow
He battled, conquered, failed, and fell—
    Full twoscore years ago

They've wrapped him in a noble sheath,
  The flag without a fleck;
They've borne him from the grave beneath
  The walls of old Quebec.

The land he left in doubtful strife
  Has triumphed, free and blest;
And him that died to give it life
  His people bear to rest.
The bride he kissed a blooming lass
  Is wrinkled, old, and gray;
She hears the drums; she sees him pass;
  She droops and swoons away.

.   .   .   .

Loud boomed the bell of high St. Paul's
  From out the hollow dome;
And thus below those ivied walls
  Montgomery came home.

A DREAMER

Here lies a little boy who made believe;
   Who found in sea and city, hill and star,
What wise men said were not; who loved to weave
   Dream warp and woof more fair than things that
        are.
He made believe that heavy toil and stress
   Were only play, and sang the while he wrought;
He made believe that wealth and fame are less
   Than faith and truth—that love cannot be bought;
That honor lives; that far beyond the goal
   That lures our eyes, to nobler ports we steer;
That grief was meant to forge the living soul,
   And death itself is not for men to fear.
At last he made believe his play was played;
   A kindly Hand the darkening curtain drew.
So well he made believe he nearly made
   The world believe his make-believes were true.

DUTCHMAN'S QUIRK

THE more modern streets in the upper section of Manhattan are laid out with an impartial regularity that is unquestionably convenient even if painfully inartistic; but the older ways of the lower city often ramble with a delightful lack of responsibility. There is a story in every crook and curve of these old highways and byways. One bend is due to the whim of the pioneer cow who trod out the path which established the line of the street; another is accounted for by the course of a forgotten stream that still runs, deep underground; while yet another tells of some old farm wall, building, honored landmark, or other token of vested rights that the early roadmakers dared not desecrate or disregard.

The following ballad tells the true history of the sudden turn that Broadway takes at Tenth Street —the curve known as "The Bend at Grace Church."

DUTCHMAN'S QUIRK

BROADWAY reaches northward from fair Bowling
    Green
Direct as an arrow-flight, flexureless, clean
        And certain of line
        As the trunk of a pine
(And would that a rod of its frontage were mine!)
        Quite suddenly then,
        At the street numbered "Ten,"
Above a great warehouse of laces and shawls,
Just south of a chapel with gray Gothic walls,
        It leaps to the west
        Like a roadway possessed!
        In flagrant defiance
        Of Reason and Science,
Macadam and Telford and Byrne, and the laws
Of wise Roman roadmakers. . . . Hear ye the
    cause!

Old Hendrick Brevoort, in—what matters the date?
In days that are gone, held a goodly estate—

A "bouwerie" termed in the speech of the Dutch
(His neighbors were Stuyvesants, Banckers, and
    such);
And there with the hoardings of toil and frugality,
Lived at his ease and dispensed hospitality.

With head in the heavens, deep-rooted in earth,
A tulip-tree, mighty of burgeon and girth,

So stately and proud,
Wide-branching, great-boughed,
O'ershadowed his lawn with an emerald cloud.
'Twas Hendrick's delight in the cool of its bower
To smoke and to ponder from hour to hour
With tankard at knee;
"For, truly," said he,
"Of all friends, the very best friend is my tree
That never provokes me and never deceives,
But echoes my thoughts with the sigh of its
leaves."

The Mayor and Council had sanctioned a plan
To straighten the roadways that rambled and ran
Cross-hatching our isle
In a wonderful style—
(Those happy old lanes!)—so they summoned a
file
Of axmen with axes and chainmen with chains
And hardy surveyors of mountains and plains
And gave them instructions,
In spite of all ructions,
To follow the chart
Nor ever depart
A hair from its guidance; regardless of mart

Or hovel or mansion, to hew out the way;
Whatever the damage, the city would pay.
Forth sailed that trigonometrical band
To further the work that the Fathers had planned;
　　　And strictly obeying
　　　The rules of surveying,
Invested with powers that challenged gainsaying,
They carried the roadway o'er high land and low,
Direct as the flight of a bee or a crow,
　　　O'er meadow and lot,
　　　Through palace and cot,
By scenes that were seemly (by wiles that were
　　　not),
　　　Through acres of flowers
　　　　And bird-haunted covers
　　　And byways and bowers
　　　　Once sacred to lovers,
Though housewives defended beleagured dominions
Or voiced from their doorways unfettered opinions
Of levels and transits and government minions—
Though cattle protested from buffeted sheds,
Though turnips and cabbages rained on their
　　　heads,
　　　Though farmer boys fought them,
　　　Though maidens besought them,

They followed their map, undismayed, till it
    brought them
To Hendrick Brevoort at the foot of his tree. . . .
What! Yield up his friend to the axman?
    Not he!
He called out his neighbors, the Blauvelts, the
    Raynors;
They stirred up their vassals and sturdy retainers,
Their tenants and servants, white, yellow, and
    black—
Dirck, Chuffee, and Hubert, Claes, Mingo, and
    Jack—
Both merry young springalds and crusty curmud-
    geons
With ax-helves and pitchforks and scythe-blades
    and bludgeons,
        Resolved to defend
        To the bitterest end
The right of a Dutchman to stand by his friend!

The Knights of the Sextant yet sought to prevail
With promise of riches or threat of the jail;
But, finding old Hendrick perverse or obtuse,
They drew off their army and patched up a
    truce.

Brevoort left the tree in the keep of his horde
To make good in law what he held by the sword.
       He called on the Mayor,
        The City Surveyor,
The Coroner, Marshal, and every taxpayer
Of substance or influence, urging his plea
Of "Woodman, oh, woodman, don't fool with
    that tree!"

Sing hey! for the hard-headed man with a
    whim!
The plan of a city was altered for him!
       The highway led straight
       To Hendrick's estate,
       Then gallantly swerved
       And gracefully curved
Away to the westward. . . . The tree was preserved!
       (To chuckle, no doubt,
       At the numberless rout
Of mortals his Majesty made to turn out.)

When up through the cañon entitled "Broadway"
You're riding on business or pleasure to-day,
And suddenly, close to the front of Grace Church,
The car takes a curve with a jolt and a lurch

That loosens, mayhap,
Your hold on a strap
And drops you quite neatly in somebody's lap,
Remember, the cause of that shameful jerk
Is, just as I've shown you, a "Dutchman's Quirk!"

NEW YORK

The city is cutting a way,
  The gasmen are hunting a leak;
They're putting down asphalt to-day,
  To change it for stone in a week.

The builders are raising a wall,
  The wreckers are tearing one down,
Enacting the drama of all
  Our changeable, turbulent town.

For here is an edifice meant
  To stand for an eon or more;
And there is a gospeler's tent,
  And there is a furniture-store.

Our suburbs are under the plow,
  Our scaffolds are raw in the sun;
We're drunk and disorderly now,
      BUT—
    'Twill be a great place when it's done!

〔 287 〕

THE "CLERMONT"

ALL contemporary accounts of the first voyage of Fulton's little steamboat tell of the surprise or fright of those who saw the strange craft, breathing smoke and flame, glide up the Hudson against wind and tide. Thirty-two hours was the time of this epoch-making trip from New York to Albany, a distance of rather less than one hundred and fifty miles; but the average time of the sloops of the day between the same points was four days. The invention of the steamboat, it has been said, was in effect the discovery of not only a "shorter route to India," that quest of generations of navigators, but also of a shorter route to all the coasts of all the seas.

It is generally accepted that the small paddle-wheel steamer whose success revolutionized navigation was named *Clermont* after Clermont Manor, the residence of Chancellor Robert R. Livingston, Fulton's constant friend, and partner in his ambitious venture; though according to an anonymous and therefore negligible writer who claims to have been a passenger on the first trip, *Katherine of Clermont* was the name painted on the historic craft.

THE "CLERMONT"

A ROAR of smoke from the iron stack
  That frights the ghosts of the haunted Hollow;
A churn of foam, and a broadening track
  For all the fleets of the world to follow.

She asks no aid of the swollen sail;
  Her engines pant and her timbers quiver;
She lifts her bows to the northern gale
  And breasts the tide of the lordly river.

The round-eyed host at his tavern door
  Lets fall the pipe and the frothing flagon;
The brown-winged sloops of the Tappan shore
  Make frightened way for the snorting dragon.

The scythe-men group and the binders flock
  To gaze in awe at the floating wonder;
The red deer stamps on the basalt rock
  And bounds away to the Hill of Thunder.

A fabled road to the far Cathay
  Old Hudson sought through our western High-
    lands;
But here's the key to a shorter way
  Through all the seas to the farthest islands.

The Craftsman's hand and the Thinker's dream
  Shall bind the lands with a shortening tether;
The wit of Man and the might of Steam
  Shall draw the rims of the world together.

A roar of smoke from her iron stack
  That frights old ghosts from the haunted Hollow;
A churn of foam, and a broadening track
  For all the fleets of the world to follow.

20   [291]

GREAT IS DIANA OF THE MANNAHATTOES!

Northward! Northward! Goddess of the Tower,
  Driving back the dappled cloud,
    Bend thy golden bow.
Mignonette and violet and autumn's tawny flower
  Fill with bloom and vague perfume
    The humming ways below.

Down from his mountains Hudson rolls away,
  Pouring forth their balsam breath
    Upon our jaded strands;
Eastward, westward, southward to the Bay
  Rock like bare November woods
    The masts of many lands.

Day lifts up the hymnal of the street;
  Night hath lamps
    Of silver for thy shrine;
Air-drift, cloud-drift play about thy feet;
  Moonlight, starlight,
    Touch thy brow divine.

[292]

Ward our gates, Wielder of the Bow!
　Guard with us a nation's weal,
　　Regent of the skies!
Crowd with keels the winnowed waves
　　That round our island flow!
Shop and mart to thee shall raise
　　The smoke of sacrifice!

THE HALL OF FAME

ON University Heights, overlooking the Harlem, stands the Hall of Fame erected to honor the names of great Americans and dedicated in June, 1901. According to a rule laid down by the founder, no names might be inscribed on the tablets of the building save those of men who were born in territory that was included in the United States at the date of the deed of gift. This regulation necessarily excluded the names of some who were largely instrumental in laying the foundations of the nation.

THE HALL OF FAME

All-Hallowe'en, A.D. 2000

A NOBLE fane of marble wall and moonlit colonnade
Looks southward from a crest that rears o'er
    Haarlem's gentle glade
To watch the jeweled city's rest in majesty serene—
The calm, strong sleep that midnight gives our
    sea-enthronèd queen—
Looks westward to the Palisades, whose frowning
    foreheads throw
An even shade upon the gleam of Hudson's silver
    flow.

The hall is filled with wondrous light and faint
    sweet minstrelsy
And softly echoed laugh and song of elfin revelry;
'Tis Hallowe'en! and once again to view those
    walls, repair
The spirits of the mighty dead whose names are
    graven there.

[295]

Within is mirth and merriment among the chosen
    Great;
Without, a surly Porter stands to guard the sacred
    gate
Against each unelected Shade that foreign birth
    must claim;
For thus decreed the gentle soul that reared the
    Hall of Fame.

    Forward stepped a graceful sprite,
    Quick of action, straight and slight,
    Ruddy-hued, with tawny hair,
    Free of speech yet debonair;
    One round hole (ah, mortal hurt!)
    Through the neatly ruffled shirt.
    "Open, Porter! I would lief
    Greet again my noble chief,
    He whose service was my school
    First in warfare, then in rule.
    Of his dearest I was one—
    Alexander Hamilton."

Answered the Porter in sullen-voiced scorn,
"Ere I admit thee say where thou wast born."

    "Where the tropic breeze beguiles
    On the sea-kissed Leeward Isles

First I breathed. But well ye ken
All our breed were Britons then."

"To all but the home-born this portal is barred,
Hie back to thy barrow in Trinity Yard!"

A stalwart form in the Blue and Buff,
With a shot-rent sash of the silken stuff,
With shoulders squared and head held high,
A statesman's brow and a soldier's eye,
The mouth where butter wouldn't melt,
And the lilting laugh of the dauntless Celt,
Sprang up the slope in the moonlight dim
And shouted clear to the Warden grim,
"Unbar the gate, my man, for me!
Make way for Dick Montgomerie!"
(So rang that voice before his fall
On old Quebec's ensanguined wall.)

Again spake the Porter: "I know not thy worth.
Proclaim, ere I open, the land of thy birth."

"My faith and troth! yer wit is flat!
I thought my tongue would tell ye that!
In Ireland, sure, I first drew breath;
But what of birth—so long since death?"

[297]

"No foreign-born spirit may enter these walls.
Go back to thy tomb in the crypt of St. Paul's!"

"Room for the governor!" iron-jawed
Stout Peter Stuyvesant walks abroad,
Quitting his charnel in old St. Mark's,
Up through the tangle of streets and parks,
Stumping away on his wooden peg
And the high-heeled shoe of his one sound leg.
Monarch of Shadows, he governs still,
Ruler by force of a stubborn will.
Sharp and direct was the word he spake:
"Rules that mislike me I dare to break.
Open the portal, ye varlet, quick!
'Ware of the swing of mine oaken stick!
Forward, my heroes!' And, at his call,
Freely they strode through the ringing hall.
Round them the banded Immortals drew,
Hailed them as brothers and comrades true.
There, in the center, I saw them stand
Pressing their lips to the Founder's hand,
Who, with a pencil of golden flame,
Entered new names on the Roll of Fame.

THE BOOK LINE

Rivington Street Branch, New York Public Library.

Come, ye that despair of the land
   Which the Future shall know—
Who doubt what the years that expand
   In their fulness must show—
Who grasp not the thing which shall be
   When deliverance comes
To millions in bondage—and see,
   At the verge of the slums,
These foreign-born children that march
   In their hundreds and more
In sunshine and storm, through the arch
   Of the library door!

Their race? Ah, what matters their race
   To our generous Mold
Of Nations! Yet, if ye would trace
   All the record unrolled,

[299]

Take heart from the days that are dead:
  For the fathers of these
With Lief or with Eric the Red
  Braved mysterious seas,
Or followed Yermák through the snows
  Of a boreal dome,
Or gave to the eagles the foes
  Of Imperial Rome;
Or tented with David, or ranked
  In the Balkans those swords
That bulwarked all Europe, unthanked,
  From the Ottoman hordes.
Aye, old at the time of the Flood,
  Still the law is the same;
The Builder shall spring from the blood
  Whence the Warrior came.

They trail through the alley and mart
  To this Palace of Tomes—
Wee urchins, red-hatted and swart
  As their underworld gnomes,
And hundreds of quaint little maids
  Wearing ribands of green
Or scarlet on duplicate braids,
  Quick-eyed, orderly, clean,

And silent. Some take from the shelves
　　Of the volumes arow
Those legends of goblins and elves
　　That we loved long ago;
Yet more choose the stories of men
　　Whom a nation reveres—
Of Lincoln and Washington, then
　　Of the bold pioneers
Who plowed in a blood-sprinkled sod,
　　Whose strong hands caused to rise
That Temple which these, under God,
　　Yet shall rear to the skies!

THE END